Music 3–5

D0165451

This book gives information, ideas and principles for music with three- to five-year-olds that are both down-to-earth and up to date. Written in a style that is engaging and readable, it integrates recent theory and practice, illustrating the discussion with examples and ideas taken from real life.

Chapters in this inspiring and engaging book show practitioners how to:

- ▶ connect with the educational concepts and principles of using music in early years settings
- ▶ recognise and understand children's musical starting points
- ▶ foster creativity through music
- ▶ support listening and communication through music
- ▶ learn about the key areas of listening, singing, using instruments and dancing
- ▶ develop children's musical understanding
- ▶ widen opportunities for music through resources, new technologies and visiting artist projects.

Early years practitioners and students will find this a valuable introduction to music with young children. More experienced practitioners will find the contemporary ideas a source of inspiration.

Susan Young is Senior Lecturer at the University of Exeter. She also provides research, consultancy and mentoring for a wide range of early years arts projects.

The Nursery World/Routledge Essential Guides for Early Years Practitioners

Books in this series, specially commissioned and written in conjunction with *Nursery World* magazine, address key issues for early years practitioners working in today's nursery and school environments. Each title is packed full of practical activities, support, advice and guidance, all of which is in line with current government early years policy. The authors use their experience and expertise to write accessibly and informatively, emphasising through the use of case studies the practical aspects of the subject, while retaining strong theoretical underpinnings throughout.

These titles will encourage the practitioner and student alike to gain greater confidence and authority in their day-to-day work, offering many illustrative examples of good practice, suggestions for further reading and many invaluable resources. For a handy, clear and inspirational guide to understanding the important and practical issues, the early years practitioner or student need look no further than this series.

Titles in the series:

Circle Time for Young Children
   Jenny Mosley

Developing Positive Behaviour in the Early Years
   Sue Roffey

Identifying Additional Learning Needs in the Early Years: listening to the children
   Christine MacIntyre

Understanding Children's Development in the Early Years: questions practitioners frequently ask
   Christine MacIntyre

Observing, Assessing and Planning for Children in the Early Years
   Sandra Smidt

Encouraging Creative Play and Learning in the Early Years (forthcoming)
   Diane Rich

Essential Nursery Management: a practitioner's guide (forthcoming)
   Susan Hay

Learning and Playing Outdoors (forthcoming)
   Jan White

Thinking and Learning about Maths in the Early Years (forthcoming)
   Linda Pound

GEORGIAN COLLEGE LIBRARY

25 0201(00)
$ 34.40

Music 3–5

Susan Young

Library Commons
Georgian College
825 Memorial Avenue
Box 2316
Orillia, ON L3V 6S2

Routledge
Taylor & Francis Group

LONDON AND NEW YORK

**NURSERY
WORLD**

First published 2009
by Routledge
2 Park Square, Milton Park, Abingdon, Oxon, OX14 4RN

Simultaneously published in the USA and Canada
by Taylor & Francis Inc.
270 Madison Avenue, New York, NY 10016

Routledge is an imprint of the Taylor & Francis Group, an informa business

© 2009 Susan Young

Typeset in Bell Gothic and Perpetua by
Florence Production Ltd, Stoodleigh, Devon
Printed and bound in Great Britain by
Antony Rowe Ltd, Chippenham, Wiltshire

All rights reserved. No part of this book may be reprinted or
reproduced or utilised in any form or by any electronic, mechanical,
or other means, now known or hereafter invented, including
photocopying and recording, or in any information storage or
retrieval system, without permission in writing from the publishers.

Every effort has been made to ensure that the advice and
information in this book is true and accurate at the time of going to
press. However, neither the publisher nor the authors can accept any
legal responsibility or liability for any errors or omissions that may
be made. In the case of drug administration, any medical procedure
or the use of technical equipment mentioned within this book, you
are strongly advised to consult the manufacturer's guidelines.

British Library Cataloguing in Publication Data
A catalogue record for this book is available from the British Library

Library of Congress Cataloging-in-Publication Data
Young, Susan, 1951–
    Music 3–5 / Susan Young. – Ed. 1.
        p. cm. – (The nursery world / Routledge essential guides for
    early years practitioners)
    Includes bibliographical references and index.
    1. School music – Instruction and study.   I. Title.
    II. Title: Music three–five.   III. Title: Music 3 through 5.
    IV. Title: Music three through five.
    MT1.Y655 2008   372.87–dc22
    2008005454

ISBN10: 0–415–43056–9 (hbk)
ISBN10: 0–415–43057–7 (pbk)

ISBN13: 978–0–415–43056–2 (hbk)
ISBN13: 978–0–415–43057–9 (pbk)

For Charlie

Contents

Acknowledgements

With thanks to the many children with whom I have played, sung, danced and talked, and to their parents who have given permission for observations and studies. Sincere thanks as well to the friends, colleagues, practitioners, teachers, musicians and many others with whom I have had the privilege of working and from whom I have learnt so much. This book draws in particular on recent work undertaken as part of Birmingham early years projects led by Nancy Evans and Cynthia Knight and funded by Birmingham Children's Services.

To begin

What might an ideal musical setting look like?

Let's imagine.

*   *   *

Sam, four years old, arrives early at a children's centre with his mother. Both wonder who the visiting artist will be this week. As they near the entrance, they hear a traditional music band playing in the entrance area. Sam and his mother stand and listen for while; both of them sing along with a song they know; they chat to friends, Vijay and his father. The band is from around here. When it's time to say goodbye, Sam checks he has 'Singin' Ted' safely in his rucksack. It was his turn to take Singin' Ted home for the weekend. He's pleased that he managed to persuade his Dad to sing *Yellow Submarine* with the silly words he makes up for journeys in the car. They added it to the growing collection of family songs that Singin' Ted can record and play back.

As he goes into the main room, his friend Vijay has already got out the drums and set them out in a circle. This is their favourite activity this week and Vijay and he have been watching a recording of a tabla player who was in the centre a couple of weeks back. They like to play along with the DVD. Their educator, Niki, has been watching this play activity develop and today, included in her planning, is a reminder to spend time to listen intently to them. She talks with them about their playing, asking them to show her their drumming. They explain and she listens, taking notes.

Today Anna is here. She visits once a week as the children's centre creative practitioner. Last week Sam with some of the other children made up a saga with drawings, drama, singing and instrumental music. They recorded it on the class video camera. The saga involves a story of chase and danger, rescue by Thunderbirds and getting home for tea.

The children hear Niki singing a gathering song and so they collect around her on the carpet for register. Then she introduces a new song to them, singing it slowly, quietly and deliberately. She reminds them to listen to how she sings it before joining in with her singing. She asks what they would like to sing now and who will start. Kristy sings a children's TV song she knows. Today Niki asks Sam if he would be the one to choose some music from a website for drink and fruit time later in the morning and she'll help him save it on the MP3 player.

*　　*　　*

Wishful thinking? Maybe. But I hope this imaginary day is balanced carefully enough between blue-skies thinking and what is practical to set thoughts running.

For Sam? Is he being given the opportunities to develop his musical skills, understanding and interests in line with his own priorities and the priorities of our time?

His musical day ranged across listening to live and recorded music, playing instruments with a friend, singing, making up a song and story drama, and using technology. There were music links with his friends, family and with his locality; a rich diet of music to sing, play, improvise and listen to. Music flowed in and out of the times and spaces of his day. There were interactions with the adults; some as performers, some as play partners in making up story and music; some in more conventional 'teaching' moments such as to learn a song, or to be shown how to download. His day also shows that pull – but a pull that can be productive – between cultural continuity, the introduction of children to traditions of music (the conventional skills of singing, copying tabla drumming from a DVD) and the involvement of young children in activities that they have shown interest in and that fit with their current musical abilities, interests and inspirations.

Drawing these thoughts together into a list, well-conceived music experiences:

- ▶ provide many opportunities for him to make his own musical choices;
- ▶ are structured and interactive across a continuum of adult and child involvement, ranging from independent, free play

to adult-led, from individual to largish group, from active and exploratory to focused and thoughtful;
- provide different roles (performer, creator, listener) and relationships (with family, professionals, peers) and forms of participation (highly involved through to marginal);
- are based on high-quality resources, both people and things, spaces and times;
- focus on his interests, experiences and the processes of learning in music;
- encourage expressiveness and imagination;
- are flexible to allow for improvisation and encourage risk-taking and spontaneity;
- introduce him to musical experiences – including performances – of the best quality possible that are appropriate to his age and interests in content and how they are presented.

And for the educator Niki? I don't think there is anything here in her day that is very complex or difficult to achieve. There are resources, both material and human: the visiting artists and the expressive arts professional who works as one of the team at the children's centre. There are instruments, CDs, DVDs, technology. True, the resources may be pie in the sky given current budgets, but we should think big and aim high.

Niki holds on to a conviction that education should involve active, constructive and creative learning. Notice how her role is as much a planning, management and collaborating role – with other members of teams – as it is working directly with the children. She had organised with others to bring along the music band, to check with Anna, to organise 'Singin' Ted', to make sure the music resources were in order, to listen carefully to the two playing drums and make some notes about their playing, to decide on a new song to introduce this week.

What knowledge, qualities and attitudes might someone like Niki need in order to be an effective early childhood professional providing music? Here is my attempt at such a list.

For Niki to provide well-conceived music experiences she strives to be:

- convinced of the value of music in the education of young children and aware of how her personal background influences how she views music;

3

- ▶ aware of how music plays a part across the whole of children's lives and how to create continuity between their 'inside' and 'outside' musical experiences;
- ▶ knowledgeable about young children's likely patterns of development and their likely patterns of interest across all forms of musical activity;
- ▶ knowledgeable about and able to use a wide repertoire of pedagogical approaches;
- ▶ interested in a wide variety of music and interested in making musical connections with local people and places for music;
- ▶ a good listener;
- ▶ a good communicator, able to work with other professionals, and with a strong sense of empathy with others;
- ▶ alert to equal opportunities in terms of gender, race, religion, ethnicity, age and sexual orientation;
- ▶ open-minded, continually questioning her practice and ready to be challenged, or to take risks.

The ideas on these two lists – the one for Sam and the one for Niki – are what this book is about. The four chapters of Part 1 set the scene for early childhood music education now and then go on to consider aspects of pedagogy, musical childhoods and musical neighbourhoods. The five chapters of Part 2 look at the different dimensions of practice: listening, using voices, instruments, dancing and translating music into other media to develop children's understanding.

Before we move on: this is a book about music, but for children who dance, dramatise, vocalise, verbalise, play with toys, their friends, the adults around, or play on equipment and in and out of spaces, the separation of activities and experiences into single strands of activity such as 'music' makes little sense. It is we as adults and the curriculum documents we devise that continue to see music as a separate area of activity. Throughout the book I try not to trap children's activity in a box marked 'music' but instead try to convey how, for young children, it is woven into their lives, and woven into their expressive and playful activity.

PART 1

CONTEXTS

First things first

This is a 'slow book'. There are 'fast books' of activities and songs, quick-fix tips, lists, guidelines and ready-made lessons. Fast books of practical activities and teaching ideas promise quick solutions and corner-cutting but often leave the underlying principles and values untouched. This book is about the processes and principles behind music with three- to five-year-olds, rooting these in theory when it is useful to do so and then going on to discuss approaches to practice that build on those principles. It is a slow process, but the fundamentals that underpin music education practice need to be regularly reconsidered, particularly in times of rapid change – such as the present.

Today's young children are living in worlds that have changed, bringing new uncertainties and new demands. The changing nature of family life and new technologies in the home impact directly on young children's lives. Wider social, economic, ecological and political changes have a less direct, but no less significant, influence. Approaches to early childhood music education are slow to change. Methods conceived in the first half of the last century still have a strong influence on practice now. Not that they necessarily need to be abandoned – just thoughtfully reappraised in the light of contemporary times.

The three- to five-age phase, which is the focus of this book, is, in itself, a time of considerable change for young children. Typically three-year-olds move on from forms of home, childminder or day care into a preschool or nursery class, often with part-time attendance and mixing this with other forms of care. They then move on, barely a year later, to a reception class. The reception class is usually part of a larger primary school, drawing children into the formality and structure of primary schooling. Today's children have to become adept at managing transitions between the different places where they are cared for and educated. So many shifts mean that it is particularly important that we think of music in the context of their whole lives, childhoods lived at home and within distinctive localities. Later chapters take up these themes.

WHY DO MUSIC?

Why do music anyway? In a recent project that I was involved in, it was interesting to discover, through interviews, that those participating held quite different beliefs about the purpose of the music they were providing for the young children in two London children's centres. The project included professional orchestral players and, for them, although they joined in playing musically with the children, the real aim was the first steps on a road to formal music learning. They were looking for a spark of special interest among individual children or were concerned with what they perceived to be the first stages of learning formal musicianship skills. For the early childhood music specialist, music was something for all the children. Her commitment was to develop children musically in the widest sense. She was concerned to draw them equally and positively into the experiences she provided. For the early childhood professionals, music was, in the main, synonymous with singing, so some of the other playful and improvisatory activities perplexed them. Beyond that they were interested in how music could support children's development in other areas, mainly in social skills, communication, concentration and language. So, although collaborating, each was working with a different mindset. The result was that they orbited around one another, never tussling over these fundamental issues and never quite appreciating one another's aims and purposes.

The practitioner's focus on music for its benefit to other areas of children's development reflects the current educational climate. Early childhood education, generally, has become linked to instrumental purpose and the dominant message is that the goal of education is the achievement of competence in the core areas of literacy and numeracy. It results in pressures to formalise and accelerate children. The purposes of education are much more down-to-earth and achievement-focused, and much less about ideas of the good life and what is deeply important and worthwhile. I have some old early childhood music education books from the 1960s and 1970s and the idealism – although ringing quaintly in our ears now

– shines through. These days music is not closely linked to the current goals of education and therefore is 'useless' and difficult to justify. What often happens is that its purpose is linked with things 'use-full', so that arguing for music in terms of its ability to support children's social skills, their language and so on is what dominates. It is in this climate, incidentally, that I think the practice of Reggio Emilia holds out a beacon of inspiration for creative, artistic activity in times when inspiration is in short supply. We will return to talk more of Reggio Emilia practice in the next chapter.

I am not pessimistic, however. First, because I think early childhood professionals have held on to some important principles and values of play-centred practice. Their influence in the Early Years Foundation Stage curriculum ensures learning through play, promotes creative and imaginative activity, and promotes approaches that start with the children's competences and interests. There is a way to go before these are translated into music education practice, which still holds on to some conservative versions of practice. And these outdated versions infiltrate the curriculum documents so that the points that pertain specifically to music sit awkwardly and confusingly within the creative development strand they are primarily written into. But more of this too, as the book unfolds.

Second, I think that early childhood practitioners have an instinct for some of the important things about music. This is best explained via an example. I recently spent two days with teachers and groups of nursery and reception children on visits out to a theatre. Songs were sung on the bus when there were waiting times (of which there were several), when the children needed to wind down, when they were having fun to heighten the moment and when they were tired. The songs were being used and enjoyed for the present. We all use music in our lives to relax, to entertain ourselves, to liven up a dull moment. The early childhood settings are places for music, just like any other. I frequently hear music's place in early years justified because 'it is fun' or 'they love it', which I take to mean this understanding that music's value is because it is pleasurable and uplifting. This is so, and rightly so.

Third, I am optimistic because the children's centres are new kinds of places for young children, offering more flexible forms of provision and serving specific localities. There is enormous potential for arts organisations, cultural centres and arts professionals to find ways to work with children through the framework of the children's centres. As teams of multi-agency professionals come together to provide for young children in the children's centres, the ideal is for one of the professional team to be a creative practitioner – whether someone specialising in performance or visual arts.

WHO DOES THE MUSIC?

Young children's music education – and by this I mean education in its broadest sense of all learning experiences – is spread across the whole range of different contexts from home, the home of carers and extended family members, early childhood settings, community and cultural centres and, among the different people, family, friends, early childhood professionals and community artists. So, in this sense, all these people have a hand in young children's musical upbringing. However, this is a book about music in the Foundation Stage, which puts it in the hands of two groups of practitioners: the general early childhood practitioners and those music professionals who offer early childhood music. The second group have often re-routed themselves professionally from other spheres of activity, such as instrumental tuition, primary or secondary music teaching, community music and music therapy. They either specialise in the early years or it is part of a portfolio of activity.

The variety of different professionals with different backgrounds, qualification routes, priorities and allegiances, sometimes to certain methods or philosophies, makes the whole field complicated. And complicated, too, to address in a book such as this. For, if I address early childhood educators alone, it ignores the fact that there are increasing numbers of professionals offering music in early childhood settings. It is a rapidly growing field. But if I address those music professionals alone, it neglects the general early childhood practitioner. I have endeavoured to write in a way that is relevant to everyone but there may be places where the discussion inevitably leans a little one way or the other.

While the diversity of practitioners being drawn into working in early childhood music is to be welcomed, it also raises some problems and concerns. Chief among these is the absence of a proper, preliminary professional qualification to equip practitioners to work in music with young children. A recent influential research project into the effectiveness of preschool provision – overall provision, not just in music – has shown that the prior qualifications of staff are critical in ensuring good-quality practice. In the absence of any qualification requirements, practitioners, whether general or specialist, tend to be largely self-taught, developing their own formulae for 'what works for them' based on experimentation and ideas picked up in an ad hoc way from a range of sources. Those offering early childhood music as specialists may enjoy a high level of autonomy and independence, are outside any kind of regulatory system and are rarely challenged on what they do.

Short courses in early years music abound and are well attended. The ever-present use of the term 'training', however, implies a fairly straightforward process of being instructed in how to do something practical – a set of procedures, rather than the complex, subtle self-development of 'education' or 'professional learning'. Behind the term 'training' and the plethora of short courses lie hidden assumptions: the notion that working with young children is uncomplicated and simple and, being facetious, that it is simply a question of knowing a few cute children's songs and having a few activities up your sleeve.

The problem too is that 'training' drives a wedge between practice and theory. A training course is definitely concerned with practical activity.

A PLACE FOR THEORY

Those of us working with young children in music will all have 'working theories' – sets of ideas about the value and purpose of music for young children, how young children learn in music and how activities should be presented and structured. Quite often these remain largely below the surface, are taken for granted and are unexamined. Some even hold the view that theory somehow gets in the way, that it threatens the naturalness or intuitiveness of what they do. This is, in itself, of course, a theory for practice. If this book aims to be about the underlying principles and values of music education – as well as what they might look like in practice – then we should search for good ideas from theory to help in the process of exploring principles, appraising them and looking for alternatives. Theory can suggest directions to explore and can give confidence to try out new things.

That said, there is comparatively little research into early childhood music – not if viewed across early childhood as a whole, or music education as a whole. From both directions it is neglected. Music education research mainly focuses on children of secondary school age. Early childhood education tends to focus less on specific subject areas and to take broad, general foci. Music is considered marginal and the preserve of specialist practitioners. As a result, early childhood music education research – and the theories that might evolve from it – is in short supply and what there is tends to be mostly small-scale studies.

There are, as I see it, three important strands of research activity that carry serious implications for how we conceive of young children musically and, therefore, how we conceive of educational practice. The first of these is children's spontaneous, self-initiated musical activity either as singers or in playing instruments (Davies, 1992; Pond, 1981; Young, 2003a). These studies have mostly taken place in early childhood settings when children were playing freely. The second is children's participation in playground singing games and rhymes, which, although three- to five-year-olds are on the fringes of, watching and just beginning to join in such activities, nevertheless has implications for music education practice (Marsh, 2008). The third, and most recent, is an interest in children's musical activity at home. Television and radio and the music they bring into the home have been part of musical childhoods for many years now, but the recent influx of new technologies and the popular media they bring with them is profoundly changing the nature of music for young children. These strands of research, taken all together, show what children are doing of their own motivation and are therefore capable of. Findings and ideas from these areas of research will resurface in the chapters that follow. But each of them highlights different shortcomings in the way that music is generally provided for young children in educational settings, so I wanted to introduce them here briefly in order to set thoughts running.

To cut a long story short – and it is a long and very interesting story – time and time again these areas of research show that we expect too little of children in the versions of practice carried in curriculum guidance and activities books. For example, when children play instruments, far from being the random, noisy explorations they are assumed to be, careful watching and listening reveals the patterning and structuring underlying their play. When children sing spontaneously and make up songs – singing that hardly gets heard let alone listened to with careful attention – they lyrically and creatively blend language, movement and melody. When children join in playground singing games with their friends, they are not only pulling in all manner of musical material, they are creatively integrating it, transforming and making it their own. The musical complexities of many of these games belie the simplicity we assume children's singing games to have and on which many conventional models of music education practice have been constructed. When five-year-olds are tapping four-square rhythm patterns in the classroom but partner-clapping complex cross-rhythms in the playground, we need to rethink what we are doing. How does five-year-old Kristy, whom you will meet in Chapter 3, spending every morning singing boy-band songs at home with her karaoke set as she gets ready for school connect with her singing in school?

What we learn from these studies is that children are highly motivated to make music; they have potential for music and fundamental capacities to perceive and create musical units or small structures, to listen perceptively, to join musically with others. Children's musicality does not spring from some inner, innate pure source as some notions of children's musicality seem to imply, but neither do they start out as blank sheets needing to be taught everything from minimal starting points and building upwards – as many methods imply in their activities and programmes. It is better thought of as a proclivity, a potential for music that locks on to every possible source for musical activity and interest around them, avidly and actively soaking it up – and doing this from birth onwards (even prenatally, as babies are listening while still in the womb). Children exploit everything they can; their voices, their bodies, the playthings around them, friends, family members, music they hear on TV, out shopping, at the temple all present different opportunities for music. Their music arises from engaging with the people and things around them, turning the possibilities they hold into active music that they then go on to play around with and be inventive with. And this is not a passive process of absorption but a process in which children are active, turning it into something of their own. It is in this active process of appropriation that musical activities are importantly tied into their emerging identities – as it was with our own identities too.

STARTING WITH OURSELVES

The notion of musical talent has been devastating to children's opportunities in music – to children in the past, many present children and on to future children unless we try to break the cycle. Many, many adults have been educated out of feeling that they are musical, creative and imaginative. At the very least, as educators, we should be determined to do something about this perpetuation. This means unpicking the concept of 'musical talent' and recognising how it worms its way into how music is seen in our society, our education system and in our perceptions of ourselves and others as musical.

This issue is so central to music education that it deserves careful attention. Here is a prime example of how good ideas from theory can help the process of rethinking. Carol Dweck (2000) talks about 'discourses of ability' and suggests that there are two opposing views of ability. The first is that ability is more or less fixed, a gift of the gene fairy, which effectively means you either have it, you are musical, or you don't have it, and you are not musical. The other, the 'incremental view' sees musical ability more as something that can be acquired, can be learnt. Carol Dweck has shown that cultures that hold on to the 'in the genes' belief tend to undermine learners' resilience, making them feel inadequate and anxious, leading to avoidance. Whereas cultures that hold on to the 'music is learnable' belief tend to encourage an approach to learning that is more resilient – and persistent in the face of setbacks. So powerful is the 'discourse of ability' surrounding conventional music education in our society that even those who have supposedly achieved and been successful still feel doubts and anxieties about their musical ability. Therefore, understanding this and changing the discourse of ability will be an important start in conveying a view that music is 'learnable'.

The idea that musical ability is something either you have or do not have influences how music education is perceived. There is a fundamental problem. If music is not 'learnable' then it is not 'teachable' and so can never be anything more than a diversion, mild and entertaining. Just linking back to something I mentioned earlier, it is also the reason in my view why music is so frequently and so easily diverted to support other areas of learning, since it is difficult to conceive of learning within music as intrinsically achievable for all.

The idea that only some are musical is being challenged by ideas that, while some may have a greater propensity than others, as in all areas, it is in reality the advantages and opportunities in people's lives that have made the biggest difference. It is these advantages, or opportunities for learning music, that we should focus on and concentrate on how to maximise them. As Lucy Green reminds us, these opportunities are children's experiences of music in everyday life, their delight in exploring musical ideas and making their own music, their personal identity and preferences for music, the encouragement of family and friends, their play with peers, the opportunities they encounter in the form of instruments, technology, multimedia and musical people, and a desire to make music because it is pleasurable and satisfying (Green, 2002: 210). These all affect the way that latent musicality can flourish. Here we come full-circle to the discussion earlier about children's musical potential and how it thrives on experience. The majority of early childhood educators expect songs, rhymes and rhythm games to be part of their practice and know that, within this context, they do this well. Yet they will routinely say that they are 'not musicians'. Do we want to reproduce this same situation for the children we work with, or change it?

Musical biographies

So, if music is learnable, if our sense of ourselves as musical is derived not from genes, but from past experiences, then our own biography – how we experienced music in our own lives – will powerfully influence how we feel about music now, how we feel about working in music and what we think is important for children. Some may have positive background experiences on which they can draw; memories of taking part in school music activities, of learning an instrument, vivid memories of family music activities. Some may take a strong interest in music now, with extensive collections of CDs, singing or playing music, or regularly attending music events. Some may find it difficult to relate to practical musical experience, even though they listen to music a lot in their own lives. The problem arises if our musical biography contains aspects of anxiety and negativity as a consequence of past bad experiences.

Here are some questions to reflect on:

- What is the first experience of taking part in music that you remember? How old were you? Where were you? Who were you with?
- Was it a positive or negative experience? Why was it positive or negative and how did you feel?
- How do you think about music and being musical now?
- How do you respond when you listen to music?
- When did you last go out to a music event?

Map out your musical life story.

TO SUM UP

This chapter has prepared the ground for the chapters that follow by asking some fundamental questions about why we should do music and who does it? It went on to argue for the importance of theory and then used one particular theory to suggest how we could usefully rethink ideas about musical ability.

FURTHER READING

Pond, D. (1981) 'A composer's study of young children's innate musicality', *Bulletin: Council for Research in Music Education* 68: 1–12.

Young, S. (2003) *Music With the Under-Fours*, London: RoutledgeFalmer.

Chapter 2

Pedagogy

Putting it simply, in current early childhood music education practice there are two main ways in which music is planned and provided for. One is the adult-led, performance model which focuses on the singing of songs as a whole group. The children typically gather for a music time when they join in songs that the adult chooses and leads. This may extend to instruments for the children to play, some movements or body percussion activities, but generally the adult will introduce these and probably guide the children quite precisely in how they should join in. When working with larger groups, the need to manage children in an orderly way inevitably comes to dominate the approaches. The other is the free-choice, play-centred model of children being given opportunities to discover and explore, usually in free play with instruments. Typically, the adult leaves the children to play independently and there is rarely any input designed to develop these explorations. The overall result is that there are two contrasting versions of practice, two ends of what might be imagined as a kind of continuum – the one adult-led and the other child-led – but with no pedagogical approaches that span between the two.

Both approaches are underpinned by theories of how children learn: either that they learn by direct transmission or by discovering for themselves. There has in recent years, however, been a strong shift away from both these versions of learning to understanding learning as a two-way process between those who have more experience and those who have less. Probably, adults are the more experienced, but not necessarily – it might also involve children working with children. From this view education is thought of as a form of dialogue between partners whose contributions are equally important to the process. This shift in thinking has come largely from the theories of Lev Vygotsky (1987). Vygotsky emphasised the central importance of learning as a social communicative process between those with different kinds of experience and knowledge – of give and take on both sides. Much of his theoretical work focused on the use of talk to develop children's understanding. Although talk is certainly important, for music education his theory of learning as dialogue can be drawn into the medium of music itself: making music together and sharing musical processes as a means to learning.

The chance to interact with adults as more experienced partners is not simply about directly passing on knowledge and skills, although this might well get woven into the process. Through shared activity the adult helps children to build ideas and understanding, to 'construct' from what they both contribute. The notion of learning that underlies this pedagogical approach is that it is neither passively absorbed from those who tell us, nor does it well up from inside us as a release of creativity, nor is it 'discovered' by playing with material things. Learning is understood to be an active process of constructing understanding from what all those participating bring and give. It is actively assembled from the sources available. Children constantly gather up from every opportunity and try to make sense out of all the disparate 'bits and pieces'. The adult can assist this process by endeavouring to arrange the bits and pieces so that they have more chance of joining up, so that there is some coherence and continuity between them. Therefore, through the adult's efforts the children have more chance to develop their skills and understanding. But also, and this is a kind of paradox that adds to the challenge of working to develop children's creativity, the adult should not smooth things out too much, or emphasise logic and sequence at the expense of the unexpected and divergent. Creativity arises in the unexpected, in taking a turning that is not the most obvious, in finding new combinations and possibilities. If the adult over-structures the children's learning, they have no freedom to develop their own imaginative ideas. This process of structuring is often termed 'scaffolding'. But scaffolding to me implies a quite rigid framework that builds upwards towards a goal. There might be some aspects of music where a goal is in mind – learning a song, for example. But alternative ideas such as 'co-construction' or 'shared musical thinking' allow for the possibility of the musical activity going in directions that have not been decided in advance – for creative music-making, in other words.

A key element of Vygotsky's theory is what he referred to as the 'zone of proximal development'. This is the distance between what the child can do on their own and what they can achieve with guidance or collaboration with their more experienced partners. The aim, then, becomes to assist children within this zone and to provide the support children require to do things successfully that would otherwise be just a step or two beyond them. The difficult task for educators is to decide what kind of input, when and how much. Pitch it too low, and the effort is wasted; pitch it too high, and the children are bypassed. So working out where children are now, and where they might move to next, become central pedagogical skills. It is a highly skilful way of working with children. In adult-centred approaches, when teaching music to young children is thought to be about breaking music itself down into very simple bite-sized portions to feed to children step-by-step, the task seems relatively straightforward – hence the innumerable activity ideas and curriculum books. In child-centred approaches, when learning about music is thought to be something children discover for themselves by exploring and adults should not disturb, the task is, again, straightforward.

So here is one of the central ideas I hope to convey in this book – the existing models of practice that lie at two ends of a continuum might each develop through interactive processes between adults and children (or children and children). This doesn't mean it need always be an equal balance. There will be moments when the adult may take a strong directive lead or when the child takes full lead and the adult withdraws, watches and listens. But the decision to take or relinquish control will have been made knowingly and knowledgeably, not out of habit or by chance. What I hope we arrive at as the chapters unfold is a wide repertoire of possible ways to work with children in music.

Before we move on, it is valuable to notice that these ideas of learning through communicative music, of the dialogue being a musical one, also line up with recent theoretical perspectives on music itself. From studies of music in diverse cultures, from popular, folk and jazz music studies, music has increasingly been understood as made in social processes of people playing together, or listening and dancing together. Conventional music theory casts music as a solitary, academic pursuit concerned with the inner workings of the musical sounds themselves – analysis of pitch and rhythms, analysis of structure and so on. So we can see, too, how 'music as theory' has infiltrated early childhood music education practice in the emphasis placed on children learning about the elements – the basic building blocks of music. Not that there isn't a place for these aspects –

but we need to be clear on how and why they contribute to children's musical learning.

From another direction, the relatively recent area of research into infant and caregiver interaction has demonstrated that the non-verbal processes of communication between the pair are characterised by musical qualities of melodic, phrased vocalisations and rhythmic gestures: non-verbal communication born along by processes that are essentially musical in nature. From all these directions it is a small step to see that, if music is something as made between people, if music is deeply rooted in young children's communicative abilities from babyhood, then it makes sense to conceive of educative processes that are essentially about the social processes of music-making. And when music is made between people, when it is shared, it is animated, it becomes expressive. Children don't express 'ideas' that arise from solitary minds; they join in musical experiences with others so that the very act of sharing music fosters their musical imagination and creativity.

PEDAGOGICAL SKILLS

If the actions of adults in interaction with children are now understood to be so crucial to children's learning, then it is important to develop a high level of awareness of these pedagogical techniques and how they might be applied. So in the sections that follow I now discuss these in some detail.

Eliciting and prompting

'Eliciting' is about planning the times, spaces, groupings, things and people to provide situations in which children are motivated to make music and to make music in ways that are designed to suit their capabilities and interests. I like the term 'eliciting' because it suggests planning situations that invite or draw in the children to participate. Setting out the same group of well-worn instruments may not be very motivating. Sitting on the carpet and starting to sing a gathering song may elicit considerable interest and quickly draw in a whole class of children, motivated and ready to sing. Thus, some eliciting environments will be designed for children to make music with a high level of independence; some will be designed with a high proportion of adult guidance and input.

Planning clearly includes anticipating how the children will participate. Some prompting may be required as the activity starts up, to give impetus or to direct or redirect it. This might be as simple as offering beaters on an instrument or providing more structured prompts or stimuli such as starting to play drum rhythms or putting on a CD. Think back to the imaginary day at the beginning of the book and to how Niki, the early years professional, had planned a range of situations to motivate the children's participation.

Listening and watching

The shift to understanding learning as processes of two-way interaction between adults and children places extra demands on practitioners being very aware of what the children are doing individually. This information tells us what input to make. Then pedagogical interactions are not left to mere chance or habit. Listening, watching, interpreting and deciding become central activities. There is already a strong emphasis on listening and watching in general early years practice that is not marginal to the pedagogical process but central to it. In adult-led music work it is probably true to say that there is much less of a tradition of listening and observing intently – at least nothing more than a casual unstructured noticing. It is important to see observation not as a luxury extra, nor as a follow-on to be written up afterwards, but as far as possible an integral and ongoing part of the process. For music this creates particular challenges. If the adult is making music with children, actively singing, playing, dancing, then it's not so easy to have post-it pad in hand or to balance a camera on one knee – but more of the practicalities later.

It is not only the practical complications that make listening into children's music-making a challenge. It is, as well, because there has been so little tradition of listening to children's music, of holding high expectations of its worth and knowing how to make sense of it. Recall in Chapter 1 how I talked about the notions of music as a specialist subject, the idea of musical talent worming its way into every aspect of how music is provided for. Here is just one example of how this operates to deny value to children's own self-generated musical activity. In the chapters that follow, I will give descriptions of children's likely patterns of interest that have been arrived at from some research studies, because these can provide helpful frameworks for interpreting and making sense of what children do musically.

And there is another subtle but very important point to add. When we are listened to intently, respectfully, empathetically, it is empowering. Just the very act of being listened to feeds back into what we are doing, how we feel about what we are doing, so that it grows and develops. Listening is, just of itself, a valuable pedagogical strategy.

Interacting and structuring

So the challenge of working with children in music is in making judge-ments, often snap judgements, about when and how to join in – how to connect up what you sing, play, dance, say, draw, gesture, with what the children are singing, playing, dancing . . . often termed 'intervention'. But to intervene implies something abrupt to me, as if interrupting the flow or rhythm of an activity rather than smoothly joining in, picking up the pace and dynamic set by the children. Pause and reflect for a moment here. Mostly we expect children to join in with our music, a song we have started up, or live or recorded music, rather than we, as adults, trying to join in with them, with their music. This turnabout may be difficult to imagine, so let us hear about the work of two experienced practitioners.

Joanne Rutkowski and Yun-Fei Hsee are early childhood music educa-tors working in the US and Taiwan. Together they are researching and developing ways of working with children in group activity based on principles drawn from Vygotsky's work and notions of scaffolding (Hsee and Rutkowski, 2006). Their aim is to work with groups of children in ways that offer much more flexibility for the children to contribute their own ideas than adult-led, large-group activities conventionally do. They demonstrated their approach in practice. Joanne clapped rhythm patterns for the children to echo – a well-known activity. However, after a few turns, she paused, waited without a word, quite still. After only a brief moment, some of the children contributed their own rhythmic patterns without bidding. She copied one pattern and the other children echoed as before. This continued with various children offering pattern ideas. If an idea offered didn't 'fit' quite so well with the tempo they were all holding or with the length of the four-beat gap, Joanne could straighten it out rhythmically as she imitated it. In this way rhythm patterns were invented, shared between her, individual children and the whole group. Joanne could be sure she was taking up patterns that matched the children's current skill levels but at the same time 'feed in' her expertise to lead the children on. Moreover, because the children could, for the

most part, join in successfully, even though her contribution was sometimes needed to tweak the rhythm, she could be sure the activity was well
pitched. Too often these kinds of musical games are merely consolidating
what children can do already rather than moving them on.

The lesson continued with some recorded music to which the children
moved freely. Both Joanne and Yun-Fei participated in the dancing,
imitating the movements of certain children when they came within their
orbit and, if it seemed welcome, joining in to make a partnered dance
with them. Then a song was sung and developed into improvised phrases,
again with plenty of opportunity for the children to contribute their own
ideas.

Joanne and Yun-Fei were taking an active participatory role in order
to make the activities musically accessible, and also musically coherent
and meaningful. For the song, or the rhythm activity, it meant breaking
the activities down into smaller, manageable parts so that the children
could 'get on board'. Or with the dancing it meant helping to build up
the dances by responding, by imitating the children's dance movements,
so that they started to grow into more coherent dance forms and connect
with the music. Through these various ways of co-constructing the music
with the children, the adults were making the activities more learnable
and also ensuring that the activities had developmental potential.

To clarify these processes, the adult aims to:

▶ *Imitate* the child/children's actions (singing, vocalising,
   instrument playing, moving, drama) and also offer ideas for
   children to imitate.
▶ *Assist* the children in continuing musical ideas or allow the
   children to assist others.
▶ *Prompt* new actions on the part of the child that are meaningful
   within the shared activity or allow for and take up prompts
   from the children.
▶ *Introduce* new ideas that extend or enhance, without
   interrupting or taking over the direction of the activity, or take
   up ideas introduced by the children.

Assisting and instructing

The careful observation of children will also reveal moments when the
adult recognises that one child or group of children would benefit from

some kind of direct input – assistance or instruction. Music requires specific skills: how to sing; how to handle instruments and produce sound; how to operate technology. While some skills may be picked up from the adult modelling, there is benefit in developing them by providing progressively structured activities. Again, however, these need to be well judged to be developmentally appropriate, so that they match the children's current levels of ability. While much early years music focuses on singing, for example, it is rarely conducted with children in such a way that supports their learning to sing, but for the most part consists of merely singing through familiar repertoire.

THINKING IN AND ON PRACTICE

All these processes of attentive listening and making judgements about just what contribution is the right one require the self-awareness and thoughtfulness that is often encapsulated in the term 'reflective practice'. There are different layers of reflection. Dorte Nyrop, a very experienced early childhood music professional working in Copenhagen, Denmark, has coined the term 'micro-pedagogy' (Nyrop, 2006). By micro-pedagogy she means the myriad small decisions and actions that have to be made on the spot when working with children. Nyrop's idea of micro-pedagogy, thinking on the hoof, is very similar to Donald Schön's notion of 'reflection in action'. Schön contrasted 'reflection in action' with 'reflection on action', by which he means thinking back over teaching once completed (Schön, 1987). By reflecting on practice it is possible to become more aware and conscious of micro-pedagogy – in-the-moment thinking and acting.

Working with children cannot be explained in terms of 'learning' or of 'teaching' as separate processes – or, to put it another way, cannot be focused on what the children do or the adult does without recognising that it is the active contributions of both in interaction that explains the quality of the children's experience. Even when a child is playing on a xylophone apparently quite independently, behind the scenes adults have provided the space, the time, the equipment, and have allowed for solitude. Traditions of observation in early years practice tend to focus on the specificity of the child's actions and behaviours – to be child-focused. Traditions of paperwork in early years music practice tend to focus on the plans and actions for teaching – to be adult-focused. Reflecting on practice within a pedagogy that understands learning/teaching to be a form of dialogue means that the focus becomes adult and child in inter-action.

To reflect on practice, information is needed. This may be simply a memory of what happened, written up in a log book for example. But memory can be unreliable. Evidence is more formal and reliable if it is collected in action as field notes, drawings, photos, video or audio record-ings. The processes of reflecting on practice, as an integrated part of pedagogy, are given more attention in the short sections that follow.

Focus

It is useful to decide upon a question or problem that launches and guides the collection of information and this then determines a focus and narrows the process. As a general rule, it is better to go deeper than to endeavour to collect observations from all that happens.

Selection

There are some ways of selecting (often called 'sampling' in research terms) in order to increase the focus:

- ▶ *The numbers of children*. Select a number of children to track rather than the whole group. For example, in one study, out of a group of 20 we selected six to track over 12 sessions.
- ▶ *The types and range of activity*. Select certain types of activity to focus on. For example, I focused once on children's spontaneous singing during free play. In another study we focused on just three songs and how a group of children learnt and participated in these over a series of music sessions.
- ▶ *The time or space*. Decide on a time-sampling system. For example, every ten minutes we noted down who was playing at an instrumental set-up and what they were doing.

Collection

Video is a very good medium for working with children's activity in music because it captures the sound and action of music-making. With the increasing availability of cameras, particularly digital video cameras, it is becoming easier to work with video.

I find I use the digital camera more as an aide-memoir for factual information, such as place, space, children present, equipment and so on. Still photos do not capture the music itself, so need to be accompanied by copious notes about the music taking place.

Writing observational notes of music activity as it happens is hard work and requires concentration. (Here I have in mind the continuous writing of notes, rather than the occasional jottings.) I write only on the right-hand page of the notebook, on lined paper, leaving every other line free. Then, as soon as possible afterwards, I go back through the notes and fill in gaps. Later, when I review the notes, I have the left-hand page for further thoughts and interpretations.

Description

In writing observational notes from live action or from camera recordings it is important to write in detail about what the children are actually doing, but try to avoid starting to make interpretations or judgements. One of the key principles in research is to differentiate clearly between description and interpretation. So 'Ozman bangs the drum noisily' is both bland and beginning to interpret. Whereas 'Ozman holds the beater in his right hand, high above his head and brings it down strongly on to the drum with many, slow big swings (about eight?) making a loud sound' gives much more factual information from which a picture emerges. We can interpret from this information that the strikes are likely to be loud. But to describe it as noisy banging is already moving towards an interpretation that contains a hint of negativity. The discipline of trying to write factual information helps to focus attention on what is actually happening rather than slip into subjective impression of what we think is happening.

A similar process can happen with photographic and video data. Where the camera is positioned, how it zooms in or out, how it pans are all decisions that can carry implicit assumptions about what is more important to record. The aim is to produce as unbiased a record as possible. Most importantly, the video needs to pick up what both the adults and children are doing and not eliminate one or the other. This can be difficult in larger group work without jerking back and forth or standing so far back that no detail is picked up. One answer is to video children and write detailed notes of adult activity.

Interpretation

The first stage in interpretation is to go back through the information collected, be it notes, video data or whatever, and to look at it repeatedly, 'stay with it' and avoid moving too hastily into interpretation. As I start to think through field notes, I put ideas that are beginning to move towards interpretation on the left-hand page, along with notes of what I plan to do next. With video data, if you have a simple editing software, it is possible to start reducing it to shorter clips. This helps with managing the video data and pulls out those sections that are most informative. Usually it is not necessary to transcribe any of the visual data, but it is still important to review it several times. It is surprising how things not noticed at first start to emerge from the process of looking again and again.

Drawing on relevant theories or research findings can be helpful in both focusing the process of collecting information and making interpretations. For example, if the focus is on how reception-age children are learning to sing, then models of children's singing development or theories of how children best learn could be used to help with making interpretations.

Application

Collecting, describing and interpreting the children's activity all lead to one aim, which is to decide what to do next. Increasing our understanding of children's musical activity will only be a valuable exercise if that understanding is converted into future action and influences how situations for music learning are planned for. Curricular plans, activities and materials are useful to provide suggestions for what to do next, but these must be married with decisions about what the children would most benefit from in terms of their own progress and development. Reflection on practice becomes a constant cycle of review and forward planning in order to continually develop and improve.

Interpreting and acting on interpretations involves, as well, a conscious act of thinking deeply about the assumptions and 'taken-for-granted' ideas that all of us bring with us and that inevitably frame our interpretations. To analyse, interpret and then go on to criticise and resist what is comfortable and familiar is a process often termed 'deconstruction'. We bring into this process of criticality our conceptions of children, conceptions of music, and our values and philosophies. And this involves our feelings and sense of identity too. Unsettling these aspects of ourselves where our professional and personal identities are interlinked can be helped by collaborating with others, using them as sounding boards, scrutinising practice together and debating.

It is in this process too that relations of power in terms of gender, race, class, age and how they mediate our expectations and operate to disadvantage some children in relation to others should be examined. Our aim, as in all education, is to continually search for how best to work with children to promote greater equality of experience and outcomes.

CURRENT INFLUENCES

Having given careful attention to pedagogical processes, I change tack now to look at three important and current influences on early years general practice and at how music pedagogy can learn and benefit from these influences. The first is creativity, which has recently come back to centre stage after quite a long period submerged by other educational priorities; the second is the influence of approaches from the nurseries of Reggio Emilia in northern Italy; and the third is the EPPE research project. The findings of this large-scale research project revealed some pedagogical styles that were associated with the most effective forms of preschool provision.

Creativity

Let us start with two imaginary examples. Merryfields School is putting on an end-of-autumn term show for parents, as they do every year, and the children from the nursery and reception class are rehearsing songs for the show. The children practise learning the words by rote every day, chanting them all together, and then learn the melody from the CD version that is played to them. When the day for the show arrives, the children all line up on the stage and sing their songs. Sounds familiar?

Meanwhile, at Cherry Lane, the reception class teacher is preparing an end-of-term occasion when the parents can visit the classroom to see a number of activities in progress or finished. At the end the afternoon they can listen to and watch some of the music pieces, dance and animations the children have made. Some of these are performed live; some are shown as recordings projected on to a screen.

It isn't difficult to recognise which of these examples of practice resulted in the children being musically creative rather than re-creative, and which children have been given the opportunity to exercise their musical imaginations. At Cherry Lane there were products as such, but the process of the children making their own music, dances and stories had taken priority over staging a formal showcase event. Reception teachers in both schools could probably tick a couple of early learning goals in 'creative development' from their end-of-term events, irrespective of the fact that one set of children had genuinely been involved in creative learning while the other had not.

Creative development is one of the key strands of the Early Years Foundation Stage (EYFS). However, a careful look at the EYFS guidance for 'creative development' reveals a poor fit between the general overarching recommendations for fostering creative development and the specific guidance points that relate to music. It is positive that these are collected into a mixed and blended collection of learning points and suggestions for creative practice across many areas – not as separate 'subject' areas. However, as we have seen, music is generally introduced to children in a way that emphasises conformity rather than creativity. The suggestions for practice in the guidance tend to reflect traditional practice. They move on from it just a little in positive directions, but nowhere near enough. Therefore, the recommendations for practice still lean heavily in the direction of adult-led, content-based activity – 'learn some songs from memory' and 'recognise rhythms', for example. The more creative dimensions of music are thinly represented by activities that have barely moved on from the free play with instruments activities – 'exploring sounds' for the most part. I will talk later about the emphasis on sounds rather than music, but here I pause to point out that these are low-level activities that disappointingly betray low expectations of children as musically capable. I introduced this idea in Chapter 1 with the promise that it would be a key thought running through the book. I will highlight these discrepancies in the chapters that follow in Part 2 and suggest more musically valuable ways of working.

Reggio-inspired practice

Another impetus and source of revitalisation for early years arts is being provided by the practice from the nurseries in the municipality of Reggio Emilia in northern Italy (Abbott and Nutbrown, 2001). The ideals of practice from 'Reggio', as it is known, offer a beacon in times that are short on inspiration for creative, artistic activity and when emotion and sensitivity, educating for quality of life and the good society seem in short supply.

In Reggio Emilia nurseries the expressive arts, particularly the visual arts, are promoted as a fundamental tool for learning. Adults aim to set up interesting, eliciting environments or introduce a specific stimulus – or 'provocation' as they term it. They then listen and observe carefully to see what ideas or actions begin to emerge in children's encounters with the materials and situations provided. Reflection on practice is a built-in component of their pedagogy and, significantly, it is the interactions between adults and children, between the environment and children, in line with a conception of learning as interactive process, that are the focus of their deliberations. Practice from the Reggio Emilia nurseries has received utmost attention, but in my experience of early years music practice in Italy, innovative music practice is found elsewhere, across wider regions of northern Italy.

In various parts of the UK there are exciting and ground-breaking projects based on Reggio principles in which music may be included as one of a range of art forms. Working in a Reggio-influenced way for music can pose something of a dilemma, however. All very well to have a group of ten or 20 children working with clay, or exploring a forest environment following their own lines of interest, but the same number working simultaneously on musical ideas risks noisy chaos. (There are some ways, and more of these in later chapters – but for now I generalise.) Moreover, the images of practice from Reggio are orientated around the visual arts and what children say. Typically, the documentation that presents the learning of children captures the drawings made and words spoken by children engrossed in activity. Music is time-based and invisible. It doesn't fix well in visuals or words (an idea I will come back to in Chapter 9). The result is that some of the pedagogical strategies associated with Reggio practice need more adaptation to music than is the case with other areas. Nevertheless, the principles of Reggio practice – of providing environments that are conducive to rich, imaginative and expressive musical experiences; of observing and seeking to understand what children are doing on their terms; of deciding how to lead on their activity by thoughtfully designed extensions and inputs; of interacting with children to foster their learning – are all highly valuable in increasing the pedagogical repertoire for music. It is less about emulating the work directly, therefore, and more about using Reggio, its values, philosophy and pedagogy as a lens through which to reflect on our own work.

There are two cautionary points I would like to raise. The first is that, sometimes, such a prize is put on the children's self-generated ideas and explorations, that adults can become reticent about ever directly assisting or instructing, even when it may be entirely appropriate. The other is that a strong belief in children's self-initiated activity as intrinsically creative, as special, natural and pure can lead to what is in reality quite low-level activity being overvalued. Some children, frankly, may be cruising or opting out. Musicality or creativity is not simply 'released'. There have to be certain conditions and latitudes of freedom, for sure, but there is, as well, application, focus, careful thinking, sensitivity, the gradual incorporation of learned skills, struggle even. We frequently see children really struggling to achieve something when they are fully involved. To distinguish dabbling from genuine involvement and effort is where thoughtful observation is essential. A commitment to child-initiated, child-led approaches can become as limiting to pedagogical options as a commitment to music-centred, adult-led approaches. My aim in this book is to keep the door open to all options, to encourage a wide-ranging pedagogical repertoire.

The EPPE Project

The recent large-scale and long-term research project to understand what made early years education effective, known as the EPPE (Effective Provision of Preschool Education) Project, drew attention to the types of pedagogy that were associated with the most effective forms of preschool education (Sylva et al., 2004).

What emerged from their study was the value of what the researchers say might be conventionally termed 'teaching' – the specific actions of adults designed to move children on in their learning. Their analysis of children and adults working together revealed how lifting the level of thinking occurred when a practitioner 'extended a child-initiated episode by scaffolding, thematic conversations or instruction' (Siraj-Blatchford et al., 2002). They coined the term 'sustained shared thinking' to capture the process of the adult being alert to the child's or children's interests and, together, participating in developing ideas, skills and activities. Here too, then, the findings that emerged from this research project have much in common with the understanding of learning as dialogue, as social communicative process, and confirm its value.

31

TO SUM UP

This chapter has talked about musical pedagogy, drawing the focus into what adults actually do in these moments of contact with children, elucidating these and endeavouring to move pedagogical practice on from the two poles of adult-led, music-centred pedagogies and child-led, child-centred pedagogies by providing a basis from theory and from recent influences on early years education.

FURTHER READING

Abbott, L. and Nutbrown, C. (2001) (eds) *Experiencing Reggio Emilia: implications for pre-school provision*, Buckingham: Open University Press.

Flohr, J.W. (ed.) *The Musical Lives of Young Children,* Upper Saddle River, NJ: Pearson, Prentice Hall.

Chapter 3

Musical childhoods

Kristy, aged 5, has a karaoke set in her bedroom. Every morning, before she goes to school, she plays a CD of her favourite boy-band and sings along with some of the tracks using the microphone. Her singing can be heard throughout the house. When I interview her parents they tell me how well she can sing and how much they enjoy hearing her.

Aadesh, aged 3, is looked after by his grandparents each morning, before he attends nursery school for afternoon sessions. At their house he watches a religious programme first thing in the morning and there are often Bollywood movies playing during the day. He has a small dholki (a barrel-shaped drum that is held horizontally) among the playthings at their house.

These glimpses into the musical lives of two children were collected as part of research studies in which I talked to 20 children and parents about their musical activity at home. They remind us that children live and learn in different worlds that include – as well as their early childhood setting – their homes, the homes of extended family members, friends and carers, out-of-school clubs, community and cultural centres, outings, travels and holiday places. Patricia Campbell has studied and written about young children's use of music in their everyday lives (1998). Each of these learning places is further connected to wider musical networks beamed into homes via radio, TV and the internet. How their families and the adults in their communities create musical environments and occasions contributes importantly to the children's musical experience and growth. Music is part of the fabric of life and how all the people children encounter allow for, support and encourage their participation in musical experiences will have a profound influence on their musical identities and sense of belonging to musical communities. Research suggests that parents' encouragement is one of the most crucial factors in children taking up instruments and continuing in adulthood (McPherson and Davidson, 2006). In the two cameos of family life described above, parents were supporting and encouraging musical activity. They supplied the instruments and technologies; they allowed their houses to be places – 'soundspaces' – where their children could sing, play and listen to music.

Children arrive in early childhood education with lives already well under way; with histories, experiences, preferences and opinions. This knowledge, these abilities, expectations and connections with music will shape how they approach musical activities in the nursery or reception class. Whether consciously or not on the part of the adults who work with them, the children's everyday musical experiences provide the context in which teaching begins and continues. We have some – but need more – information about home-based musical experiences and how these interact with the musical cultures of early childhood settings.

'Starting with the child' is a mantra of early years education. But in reality what is taken from children's home experiences is often highly selective. Educators look out through a small window, framed by their own priorities and, for the most part, if we are honest, seeing only what we choose to see. Although the concept of 'parents as children's first educators' is tacitly acknowledged, most of the influence is expected to be one way, with educational activities to be drawn down into the home, rather than vice versa. Thus the home is subtly 'curricularised', while the nursery practice remains unchanged.

DIVERSE MUSICAL CHILDHOODS

Contemporary musical childhoods are lived within dynamic and changing cultural contexts. The increasing movement of populations means that, in any one group of children, in many areas – particularly urban areas but increasingly in small towns and rural areas – there will be multiple cultures represented and multiple musical traditions. Some children who are newly arrived may have started life in communities that contrast markedly with what they find in their new communities. Their families may bring with them a musical heritage from their home country that uniquely defines them. Some children, alternatively, may belong to first- or second-generation ethnic minority families and move easily between different groups adapting their identity to each. Equally children belong to extended and to fragmented families, perhaps shifting between two or more homes, as Aadesh did. They may be adept at slipping between what seems to those of us on the outside looking in to be a cultural hotchpotch of languages, dress, food and music. But the children themselves experience all this as one blended whole. For these families, the music of their 'old world heritage' may emerge at religious and family celebrations. The families revitalise their ethnic identity on special occasions. So, among groups of children in early childhood settings, cultural and social diversity is to be expected.

Twenty or so years ago what became known as multicultural approaches to music education seemed fairly straightforward. Curricula expanded to include songs from far-away places, often with simple words that could be learnt by rote and from recordings of music from 'other countries'. The range of educational percussion expanded to include instruments with African, Asian and South American origins. There was perhaps confusion about whether the musical experiences were to be inclusive of the cultures present among the school population for reasons of representation or whether broadening the musical experiences of children was considered important in terms of freeing up children's music learning from the dominance of classical, Western music. Gerry Farrell, an ethnomusicologist with a strong interest in music education, once joked that if he, a Glaswegian, had migrated to India, his school might provide him with lessons on the bagpipes, swathes of plaid material draped over displays and singing of 'Auld Lang Syne'. His joke draws attention to the dangers of reducing culture to mere tokens. In interviews with multi-ethnic parents about what music is heard in their homes, their responses matched the exciting variety and diversity of contemporary music that is available now – all manner of pop music, folk, traditional and religious music.

How then to select from such an overwhelming variety and diversity of music? This is one of the challenges of music now, for everyone – how to sort, select and decide from the wealth of music available. Are there any guidelines for selecting music to use in a setting? It may be appropriate to anchor music education in the musical practices that make up the lived experiences of young children, the various subcultures to which they belong and the local musical practices in the neighbourhood. This allows the children to find continuity between home and setting and, from these anchor points, we can then allow the selection of styles and types of music to range freely, simply holding on to criteria that will ensure that opportunities for experiencing and learning about music are broadened.

What is clear, however, is that, in aiming to support, reflect and encourage musical diversity, early years professionals must call up other musical sources and resources beyond those they can provide single-handedly. This will involve ensuring that the collection of recorded music in the setting is extensive – not only sound, but audiovisual and multi-media. And it will include planning opportunities to hear and participate in live music by musicians living and working in the community. Think back to the imaginary day for music in which Niki organised a local band to visit and play.

TECHNOLOGIES FOR MUSIC

Home-based technology, and the multimedia and popular culture that it brings into everyday life, are having a profound impact on how children experience music (Young, 2007). As yet, early childhood music education has barely considered what implications these changes hold for practice.

This generation of children are growing up with an array of tech-nologies that are fluently integrated into their family lives and that they will use with ease. Surveys of families with young children carried out by Jackie Marsh showed that the vast majority have TV, radio, DVD, CD players and mobile phones (Marsh, 2005). The increasing gap between rich and poor means we need to be very alert to the fact that some children will live in families who do not have the financial means to purchase a wide range of technologies for the home. Static, heavier equipment may sit as the multimedia family entertainment centre in the main living area. Kristy's karaoke set was located in her bedroom and this marks the shift to bedrooms becoming spaces where children entertain themselves, often quite alone and for extended periods of time. From our interviews we heard of parents equipping even quite young children's bedrooms for entertainment with CD players, TVs and computer games.

Family members may have, as well, the newer multi-purpose handhelds that can be carried anywhere. Where music collections were once made up of fragile, cumbersome vinyl records, then cassettes and CDs, they can now be invisible digital playlists. Digitised music in tiny players can infiltrate the nooks and crannies of everyday life. The largest symphony orchestra can be squeezed through a tiny ear piece, or the delicate plucking of a guitar can fill an entire football stadium. Little tunes and sounds pop out of nowhere from toys, domestic equipment, phones, computers.

Music combines with other media in DVDs, games, TV, internet sites, children's toys – the multimedia cornucopia that is now part of domestic indoor lives for children. In these multimedia forms music blends and mixes with rapid, moving images, visual and sound effects, spoken and written text. Multimedia items are characterised by fast-pace changes, vivid animations and many-layered information.

A common reaction among practitioners, I find, is to reject children's everyday musical experiences together with the multimedia and children's popular culture that are part of them. Behind such a response lies an image of children as in need of protection or rescue from what are perceived to be negative influences. Such views are, unfortunately, often accompanied by implied criticisms of parents. Notions of introducing children to 'good music' and valuable musical experiences go hand-in-hand with these arguments. To ignore or criticise a significant part of children's musical experiences is surely not an adequate response. These musical experiences – and what children are learning from them – are already present in the nursery and classroom, brought there by the children themselves. What we need are thoughtful, level-headed approaches to practice that take account of them.

Gathering information

In recent projects I have carried out research conversations with children and informal interviews with parents to explore their everyday musical experiences. Although I was doing this work in a research role, there is no reason why practitioners could not include interviews with parents about their children's musical experiences beyond the setting as part of their documentation – and it could equally well be part of introductory interviews and profiling.

With the children we carried out research conversations with friendship pairs of five-year-olds. As a pair, they were more likely to be forthcoming than if we had spoken with them alone. We brought in a range of CDs and DVDs that we thought were representative of children's popular culture for that age and used these as a starting point for generating discussion.

Below is an outline of the questions we used to frame the interviews with adults. They seem quite formal set out in this way, but we used them as starting points and allowed conversation to develop more informally.

The questions could easily be adapted to a shorter or longer interview with the parents or carers of the children you are working with.

▶ *What musical resources do you have at home?*

- TV, DVD, CD, MP3 player?
- Musical instruments?
- Musical toys?
- Video games?
- Collection of CDs, DVDs, tapes, videos?

▶ *What music does your family mostly listen to?*

▶ *What music do you think your child listens to during the different times of the day – morning, late-morning, afternoon, early evening, bedtime?*

▶ *Do you sing with and to your child?*

▶ *Do you dance with and for your child?*

▶ *Do you play any instruments with and to your child?*

▶ *What songs or dances or other musical activities does your child take part in?*

▶ *Do you notice your child singing, playing or dancing on their own? And what kinds of music are they making up?*

▶ *Do you go out to events or occasions where there is music?*

Because we were, in addition, interested in ways of involving parents in the music in the settings, at the end of the interviews we also asked parents and carers:

▶ if they had a practical musical skill they could demonstrate – singing, dancing, playing an instrument, DJing, music technology;
▶ if they could send copies or tapes of songs they sing or rhymes they say for their children;
▶ if they could send in music from home;
▶ if they could bring, show and play any instruments they have.

* * *

So, to pause and pull together the various threads so far, not only do children come with skills and competences aplenty, but these are increasingly culturally diverse, complex and tied into the expanding experiences afforded by music technologies and the multimedia and popular culture they make available. The risk is that the gap between the culture of music in the early childhood setting and the musical cultures of children's lives outside the setting widens.

Questions and dilemmas

The first question to ask is, does this divergence matter? If one of the tasks of education is to extend and enrich, then it should provide not simply more of the same, but more and different. However, when I observed Kristy in school, she sang some simple songs with rhythm activities and actions that were well taught, but far less musically complex and interesting than her boy-band songs. Aadesh left behind listening and singing along to Bollywood movies and attempts to imitate rhythmic patterns of dholki playing for 'Wheels on the Bus' and tapping a steady beat with rhythm sticks. These 'educational' activities were musically impoverished in comparison with the musical activities he was participating in at home. That, I think, is one risk if we are not concerned to find out about and start with the skills and knowledge children already bring. The children are engaging with musical experiences at home and beyond, participating in singing, playing, dancing, with families and others and absorbing these experiences. Also, I would suggest that the boy-band karaoke singing is more meaningful for Kristy, and the dholki playing more meaningful for Aadesh than rhythm sticks. These musical experiences are more likely to connect up with their peer and family cultures, are more closely tied in with their identities and are more likely to be the musical activities they are motivated to continue. Another question to ask is, were the educational activities likely to extend the children's musical experiences in meaningful ways, or, as I am clearly hinting, become somewhat disconnected? Children have the opportunity to become more musical when experiences are tailored to their individual experiences, interests and needs. While some children may find relevance in the educational music experiences offered to them, I suggest some, perhaps many, may not.

You may think that three going on five is much too early in children's educational careers to be concerned with these issues, that I am finding

39

complications where none exist. Young children are biddable and enjoy singing the nursery rhymes and children's songs they know. And to look at the research and writing on issues concerned with popular music culture and on musical technology and its relationship to formal music education, the focus is all at secondary level. But Kristy and Aadesh were already active participants in musical experiences enabled by new technologies in their homes and connecting with musical cultures in the wider world – with pop groups, with music for religion, with traditional music. Their nursery and school were treating music in quite a different way.

TECHNOLOGIES IN PRACTICE

I turn now to consider how technologies for music might be integrated into educational practice. While trying to avoid being unrealistically enthusiastic about their potential, I do think there is enormous scope for using new technologies for music in early years education and creating opportunity for all kinds of interesting activity. Hopefully music technology might be seen as an ally, not as something that threatens the 'naturalness' of children's musical activity. Technologies offer the possibility of freeing up some of the limitations of making music with acoustic instruments. They can provide children with more creative, independent and open-ended ways of making music. Moreover, as briefly mentioned, children's access to technologies out of school beyond the most commonly available, such as TVs, CD and DVD players, begins to become much more uneven. So, if education has a commitment to even up the opportunities among children, then providing access to more interactive technologies beyond the simple listen, view and play may be important.

Technology for music, as I have it in mind, is defined broadly – to include computers, keyboards, CD and MP3 players, internet access, digital cameras and video recorders, microphones and karaoke sets, projectors and interactive whiteboards, mobile phones and any more that are so recent I haven't caught up with them yet. Reading through that list it is clear that many of these things are becoming increasingly part of everyday life, in and out of the educational setting. As the technology becomes more user-friendly, mobile and hand-held, as we become more experienced at using it, so it should get easier to incorporate it into practice. We've hardly begun. Examples from real-life practice are few and far between, and so this chapter must rely more on snippets than practice that is well established or researched. I hope it is an area that will receive more attention in the forthcoming years.

There are two directions to using technology. The first is to use it as a tool to simply extend what we are doing already, perhaps to make existing practice more efficient and more effective. So, for example, a whole-group singing session may include individual children singing into a mini digital voice recorder so that they can replay and listen to themselves singing and receive immediate feedback. The second direction is to think of the new musical processes, the new ways of working and thinking in music that are made possible through the use of technology. So, to illustrate this second mode, a keyboard linked to interactive software (I have in mind a specific software called *The Continuator*; see Addessi and Pachet, 2005) may allow children to improvise with themselves in ways that develop their understanding of musical phrase and structure that would not have been possible without the software. In this direction it is important to think not only of what is possible, but what musical processes and practices children are learning from everyday technology-enabled musical experience: how can that learning be used; are there any gaps that education needs to fill; what will children need for their technology-music futures?

Using technology to enhance learning and teaching might be encapsulated into three dimensions:

▶ technologies to enhance and extend making music;
▶ technologies to enable instant record and playback;
▶ technologies to enhance and extend searching, listening and selecting pre-recorded music.

Technologies for making music

There are various electronic instruments that are usable in early years settings. Keyboards are the first obvious possibility. Many children will have these at home and they are easily available. Some other pieces of equipment, such as microphones, soundmats, drum pads and karaoke sets, are available through educational suppliers. There are some interesting experimental instruments being produced; not yet commercially available but thought-provoking. A browse on the website of the Massachusetts Institute of Technology in the US reveals Beatbugs and Music Shapers, for example.

41

Some recent software developments are augmenting what acoustic instruments can do. We already have some of these softwares in the sampling equipment that can record simple patterns to repeat or several patterns to repeat in layers. Fiona, a folk violinist working with children in Bristol settings, took sampling equipment she uses in her own professional performing to work with nursery-age children. The children recorded vocally improvised, short phrases, played back as riffs (short motifs repeated over and over), and then layered additional improvisations over this background.

And music-making can extend into multimedia creations. Kathy Hinde, working with children in Somerset, assisted children to make their own multimedia videos of dance, movement and sound by sampling a vocal sound track and adding it to their improvised performances of dance and movement.

Record and playback

Instant record and replay facilities using microphone, MP3, digital cameras or video recorders – including some microphone and recording equipment made especially for early years education purposes – enable children to record what they have just sung or played and then listen immediately back. Opportunities for instant playback are very valuable in allowing the children to revisit, appraise and talk about the music they have made. Simple pattern-sequencing software, some of it downloadable from websites, allows the recorded music to be played around with and moulded into new versions. So, for example, some children recorded vocal sounds and then replayed them at a much slower pace, so that the sounds growled at lower pitch, or speeded them up to squeaky chirpings.

A group of musicians working in Birmingham children's centres has been exploring the potential of allowing children to review recordings of their musical improvisations taken as digital camera movie clips. They either use a laptop or replay them through an interactive whiteboard. Thus children not only have the opportunity to review and talk about their music-making, they can go on to sing, play or dance, adding another layer to the music they have made.

Search, listen and select

Using digital music banks online, selections of CDs or ready-made selections downloaded on to MP3 players, children can access, search, listen, download, share and select music for various purposes. In this way children have access to greatly increased sources and repertoires of music. The ability to find, search and sort larger quantities of information is one of the skills children will need to be music users of the future.

TO SUM UP

This chapter has introduced the idea of musical childhoods, suggesting that the musical experiences of young children in the setting should be understood as just one small component of wide-ranging experiences across the whole of young children's lives. These are times of rapid social, cultural, economic and technological change and the nature of music and musical experiences for young children in their lives beyond the setting are strongly influenced by these changes. I have suggested that early childhood music needs to think carefully about how to take account of the changing nature of children's musical experiences, in particular home entertainment enabled through new technologies. Some ways in which early childhood music education might develop through the incorporation of technologies to enhance or extend music were mentioned.

FURTHER READING

Campbell, P. Shehan (1998) *Songs In Their Heads: music and its meaning in children's lives*, Oxford: Oxford University Press.

McPherson, G.E. (ed.) *The Child as Musician: a handbook of musical development*, Oxford: Oxford University Press.

Smithrim, K. and Upitis, R. (eds) *Listen To Their Voices: research and practice in early childhood music*, Toronto: Canadian Music Educators Association.

Chapter 4

Musical neighbourhoods

Headteacher Susan Rowe and deputy Susan Humphries, working at an infant and nursery school in southeast England, describe how they:

> ensure that in each half-term block the children listen to live performances of music . . . the Ghurkha Band, internationally renowned harpists, string quartets, drummers, sitar players, brass ensembles, strolling minstrels, singers, steel bands, woodwind groups, buskers, folk musicians and balalaika players.

They go on to say how they aim to offer:

> the highest available quality to the children. [They] experience the work of a range of professional drama groups . . . they work alongside authors and illustrators, artists in residence, weavers, spinners, storytellers and a huge range of craftspeople. The work takes the children into the outside environment and into the community, and in turn it brings the community and the outdoors inside: there is a reciprocity between what is available and used in the classroom and what is available from outside the school building . . . We set out to involve the wider family group of each child, the immediate local community, the national community and the international community in our work.
>
> (Craft *et al.*, 2001: 169)

They explain that their aim is to establish a true 'community school' and to develop an education based on the principle of a dialogue between the 'more experienced and the less experienced'. Their school serves an army base and so, to invite army bands and instrumentalists to play to the children, or to go out and listen, is to embrace the characteristics and values of their locality. It integrates the school with the children's lives, their parents' lives and their neighbourhood. Inside and outside school start to merge.

Children's centres and schools are increasingly viewing themselves, not as self-contained islands, but as serving a locality and as networked into nearby groups, services, centres and organisations. This will include making links with places for music – the halls, theatres, arts centres, galleries and religious centres where music is made locally. And likewise transforming children's centres or schools into places for music, just as they do in the school above and in the imaginary children's centre that we visited in the first pages of this book. For young children, as we saw in the previous chapter, the nursery or school is just one place for musical experiences out of many such places.

STARTING LOCALLY

Any large urban area will abound in skilled and exciting performers from all over the world: African, Caribbean, South American, Asian, Eastern European. Musical traffic is free to run in all directions. Large cities and rural areas will have strong regional, local musics of folk, urban or cross-over styles. The people who make this music – sing it, dance it, play it – are often 'compelled to share it, to facilitate experiences for others to know it, to pass it on' (Campbell, 2004: 3). For children to see, hear and talk with these performers is an exciting experience, whether the performers come into the early years setting or the children go out and visit. For visits out, there is the added bonus of a trip to a local cultural or community centre.

Connecting with the music around and about is part of being proud of where we live. The challenge lies in finding and identifying these practices, choosing among them, setting up links with the performers and creating opportunities for those individuals to play a meaningful part in the children's musical experiences in the nursery or school. This kind of work is time-consuming for hard-pressed educators, but increasingly there are databases and regional organisations that can provide information. For educational settings, to develop partnerships with creative practitioners has been strongly encouraged recently as part of a move for schools and early years settings to bring together a range of collaborative professionals, pooling strengths and integrating their work to develop creative activity with young children.

It is valuable for communities to involve their less experienced members in the meaningful musical activities of its more experienced and mature members. In some communities this may happen easily. Children on the margins of Bhangra, disco or Jewish dancing at a wedding or preparations for a carnival are taking part in the activity, seeing the players and dancers, and joining in by copying as they want to and are able to. But for many children experiences such as this are in short supply and so the early childhood setting will want to broker these kinds of opportunities.

Increasingly, there are beginning to be 'in-between' spaces that are neither school nor home. Children may be taking part in community arts activities, in cultural and community centres. They are blended and more intermediate activities that are neither home-based nor school-based. These will include the many different types of more informal, open-access activities that tend to have developed around music – music or dance classes, young children's arts activities or events in open-air play spaces, community centres, museums, art galleries, theatres.

PERFORMANCE

Bringing performance artists into the setting provides live, quality, musical experiences and reminds us that music is a living art – in the 'here and now' – not just another educational tool.

Michael Keelan is a professional violinist who plays for a nearby orchestra. Without saying a word, he stood in the middle of the nursery space and ceremoniously took out his violin from its case. He tuned it and children started to gather, informally. Out flew a gypsy fiddle tune, a whirlwind of sound, trilling, sliding, from the tiniest squeakiest scrapings and scratchings to deep, scrunching sweeps of the bow. The children stood around, spellbound. He played for a long time, never speaking, but looking at the children, smiling and leaning forward with his violin as if placing this music gently into their laps.

This kind of special, peak-experience moment, when we know as an educator that something of real gain is happening, is difficult to convey in words. On this occasion the staff, very wisely in my view, held back and did not immediately question or talk to the children about the performance. Later they told me that this violin playing was reworked in the children's play during the days after. The children talked about violins in group times, they turned objects into mock violins or played 'air violin', making rapid bowing movements and vocalising in imitation of trills, slides and differently pitched sounds. Then the practitioners knew to take up this interest, finding pictures of violins and some recordings of violin music on CD to listen to. These kinds of activities develop children's awareness of musical styles and expressions that are outside their everyday experience, but can be brought within reach through direct contact and the opportunity to assimilate and play around with elements of the experience.

There are various organisations and performers specialising in creating performance arts events for young children. These include:

- ► orchestras and other similar organisations (opera companies, chamber music groups);
- ► children's theatre companies;
- ► performance groups or individuals;
- ► individual session leaders, private entrepreneurs;
- ► music service teachers;
- ► community musicians.

Many national orchestras and similar music organisations (chamber music and opera companies) have quite a long tradition of putting on concerts for young children and families. Many are now looking at how they can further adapt their work and either make it more accessible to young children and families, or take it out to early childhood settings. These are 'child-friendly' or family-friendly occasions in which the performance, its presentation, aspects of visiting the venue and how children can actively participate have been carefully thought about. Performance occasions can belong to special places – the feel of the building, the bright lighting, the squashy seats add to the overall experience. Such occasions can, as a bonus, provide a good opportunity for early childhood settings to involve families.

The performance may have to be adapted for young audiences in terms of length and pacing. However, this is not necessarily the case. It is a commonly expressed – but inaccurate idea – that children do not have long concentration spans. If the work is age-appropriate, they will engage and become engrossed for quite long periods. I have seen three-year-olds sit watching a music and theatre piece, rapt, for more than half an hour.

47

But these are usually pieces to which a considerable amount of thought has been given to ensure it is age-appropriate.

It is also not necessary to simplify the music. Hearing nursery rhymes played on an instrument is not very interesting – children want to hear the instrument played at the very best the musician can achieve, as with Michael's gypsy music. Many musicians have an intuitive understanding of how to engage their audiences of children – this is their profession after all – and how to adapt their performances for the very young. Working with some professional players from the London Symphony Orchestra, I was impressed by those who had thoughtfully selected and prepared beautiful repertoire to play, for what might have appeared the most modest of occasions with small groups of three- and four-year-olds. But as one of them said, 'the children deserve the very best I can play' – and of course he was right. Some may prefer to stick to what they have prepared; some may be able to adapt to whatever comes along. Patrick Harrild, with a cluster of four-year-olds around his knees, found that a growling lion lived inside his tuba and elaborated this in a made-up music and story piece, on the spot.

With some styles of music, taking an active part in the performance may be to dance to it, or to sing and clap along. The reverent, silent audience style of classical music is just one way to listen to music. An introduction to how the instrument is played and how the sound is produced is always of interest to the children. As is all the paraphernalia of cases, cloths and clutter that is the players' preparation. Those who are less used to young children can often misjudge how to pitch their explanations, typically saying too much and in a linguistic style that is not adapted to the age they are addressing. Rehearsing this in advance can be useful, whether you are an early childhood professional inviting musicians to check their spoken words beforehand or a musician planning a visit.

The performers need to:

- ▶ select possible repertoire in advance;
- ▶ plan how the children might be prompted to participate;
- ▶ decide if improvising to activity initiated by the children will be included;
- ▶ decide whether the children can touch and try out the instrument or not;
- ▶ plan and rehearse any talk – explanations and/or demonstrations.

Performers who can work for longer periods of time over a series of visits in an early years setting can develop their work to connect flexibly with different kinds of activity within the nursery, either taking leads from the children and seeing opportunities to develop music, playing with them using their instrument, or taking the lead for a music listening or singing session.

Trish is a folk accordion player. She is working in a large urban nursery for one afternoon a week over two terms. She works flexibly, fitting in with whatever else is going on. When the children are playing freely, she may set out instruments for the children to improvise with and join in with them. When the staff gather the children, she usually plays for a more formal song-singing session.

This kind of work requires the music professional to be experienced in terms of understanding children's music play and recognising how to join in and connect with it. With the less experienced, the early childhood professionals may need to take a more proactive role in advising and mentoring.

PROJECTS

Much early years music work, particularly that which enables musicians to work in early years settings, takes the form of short-term projects funded by external agencies. This has enabled many innovative and interesting developments in early childhood music to take place and has created opportunities for young children to work with musicians of widely varying types of expertise, thus enriching their experiences. However, although projects have many advantages, they have created a particular climate for early years music in the UK that is worth dwelling on.

Projects are typically short term, ranging from, at minimum, a one-off special event to, at best, a regular series of generously long visits over an extended period of a year or more. Usually the 'external partner' visits once a week. While the weekly schedule suits setting and artist timetables, it does not allow for the kind of sustained, day-over-to-next-day working with children that can be of most benefit. Ideas don't wait neatly until a week later, nor do they necessarily begin and end just with the once-weekly visit. Experienced partners may compensate by working in such a way that the weekly visit provides an extra impetus and leaves self-sustaining work that will continue into the following days. However, sustainable changes in practice are more difficult to achieve with one-off or short-term projects.

The setting up of arrangements and infrastructure to enable projects to take place is often complex and time-consuming and requires good all-round organisational skills. In terms of money and time, this is drawing away from activity with the children. It takes time to negotiate open-mindedly and respectfully across different priorities, expectations and working practices. The emphasis, frequently forced upon project managers by 'short termism', is to get things up and running. There is, unfortunately, rarely time for pilot projects, for full negotiation or for false starts and misunderstandings. And the all-important element of focusing on the pedagogy – how the work will be carefully designed to connect with the children – can be the last part of the structure to be considered, or neglected altogether.

In my experience, the funding climate is such that project applications are rarely negotiated in advance with the settings themselves. The first a setting may know about a project is the phone call to the manager offering the opportunity. This may be the moment that all partners need to move cautiously, ask for full detailed information and be clear on expectations.

The project culture is linked to certain kinds of idealism. To secure funding the project usually has to demonstrate that it is breaking new ground in some way and often how it is serving a wider social or educational purpose. To match current educational priorities, project aims are frequently linked to gains in the core areas, usually language and literacy, or to working with children at risk of educational disadvantage. The result is often that projects have a high element of exploratory and developmental activity within an ideological frame. Money to support activity that would build on existing successes and provide continuity for effective work is less easily available. The consequence is a plethora of short-term, dis-connected and usually highly exploratory projects.

Some project funding is specifically designed to allow the initiative to be made by the nursery or school itself. Certainly funders welcome this. While understandable that small educational settings, overwhelmed with paperwork, may not have the time, energy or expertise to write the project applications, it is a pity because then projects would arise from work that the educators have control of and could design to meet their needs. There are a number of booklets available from the Arts Council and other arts organisations that support the process of designing a project and applying for funding.

Project aims

The aim of bringing in an outside partner may be very straightforward – to give a one-off performance perhaps. But for longer projects the aims may need to be carefully considered. A clear aim gives the work direction and a framework within which roles and responsibilities can be defined. That is not to say that the aims are rigid and cannot move and bend as the work develops, but starting out with a clearly defined set of aims is important.

Establishing aims is not always easy. The tendency is to make them too ambitious and wide-ranging, particularly on funding application forms when there may be pressure to impress potential funders with what is going to be achieved.

Here are the aims of the some projects I have been involved in:

- To develop the role of a visiting musician within the organisational structures of the new children's centres.
- To study children's spontaneous music-making and explore pedagogical approaches that build on their music-making.
- To explore ways of using new technologies in creative musical activity with three- to five-year-olds.
- To explore connections between music, dance and mime, and to work towards a performance arts approach.

Each of these aims focused on the nuts and bolts of developing practical activity with children, and pinning that down quite specifically to one area. Only one of these aims leaned more towards the adult role – the visiting musician – rather than actual work with children. But even here I would argue that understanding the adult role should, if good processes of review and reflection are built into the project, still focus on what counts as good practice in working with children. And certainly in all these projects we held the nature of children's participation and their opportunity to be actively musical on their own terms as central to our philosophy.

Partnerships

There is much talk in both early childhood education and arts organisations of partnerships and establishing working relationships in multi-agency teams, but this is hard to achieve in practice and much can remain at the level of rhetoric on written documents. Like all working partnerships, it

51

requires humility and empathy to try to see things from the other person's point of view and may be challenging to our own sense of security and identity.

A key process in sharing expertise as partners is to 'cross boundaries': to enter into territory that is unfamiliar. In music projects involving early years practitioners and visiting music specialists, the early years professionals can be used to adopting a more passive and less assertive way of participating. The visiting professional, in turn, may have less appreciation of the working lives and contexts of the early years practitioners and be unaware of how they inadvertently reinforce, rather than seek to diminish, their expert status. I have been involved in a number of early years music projects in roles as researcher or evaluator. All too frequently I hear from music specialists working in early years settings that their partner practitioners seem not to appreciate or enthuse about their work. From the early years practitioners I hear that the music specialists do not understand the constraints under which they work and hold unrealistic expectations. Honest communication, both sought and given, is important to avoid these kinds of misunderstandings.

PURELY PRACTICAL

There are a number of areas that will need to be negotiated and well planned in advance if the projects and other enterprises are to run smoothly.

Information

External partners working in education often have limited understanding of the educational contexts, the changes and current priorities – and may need explicit information about curriculum design, current priorities (such as work with families or a focus on creativity) and how settings are organised. Children's centres are particularly complex organisations for outsiders to understand. Equally, external partners need to seek out this advice and not assume that they know it already or don't need to know it – things have a habit of changing frequently.

Roles and responsibilities

Being clear on who is doing what when work is planned with external partners is always important. In my experience, a mismatch of expectations and confusion about roles and responsibilities is often the reason for difficulties emerging in projects, usually part-way through. Different professional philosophies and practices on collaborative working can pose challenges for developing shared forms of practice. A review meeting held fairly early in the life of a project is useful to clarify the basic struts of the project.

Space

Plan what kind of space the visitors will work in. While, understandably, space in many early years settings is limited and not purpose-designed, artists working in these settings can work less effectively if the space is not suitable. In schools there are usually larger spaces available, but these are in demand for all kinds of activities and often tightly timetabled.

Sound environment

It is important to ensure that the external partner has the right kind of sound environment for their work. I was recently asked to work at one end of the school hall while dinner ladies set up metal tables that scraped loudly along the floor. The visiting music professional may want to do focused listening work, which is best accommodated in quiet spaces – or, equally, they may be planning for boisterous, vivid activity that will spill noise into surrounding areas.

Timetabling

Nurseries and reception classes often have quite a structured schedule to the day, particularly reception classes that are tied into whole-school timetables. The music worker may prefer to take generous chunks of time to work with children, or may wish to work through a whole session with small groups of children, one or a few at a time. And not only time, but also pace has to be considered, so that activity on one day that has really started to flow can be allowed to continue and, just as understandably, activity that falters another day can be allowed to wind up earlier. Such arrangements may call for flexibility on the part of practitioners and good communication between those working together.

Time for regular review is important and should not be scrimped or sidelined. Discussion and review time should be planned in, ideally after each visit, but realistically less frequently. An interim review at a key point in the project for a longer discussion is useful. These review meetings allow for planning ahead and, if necessary, for renegotiation of any of the practical arrangements.

Numbers, ages and grouping

Settings may often feel they want to make the most of the visiting artist and feel it is important for all children to have the opportunity to take part. Sometimes this results in long stretches of time where the external partner is scheduled to work with quite large groups one after another. In these circumstances the visitor can feel 'squeezed like a lemon' and a little exploited. Equally, artists may be less experienced at working with larger groups of young children and slightly nervous at the prospect, preferring pairs or small groups. Clearly, such issues are again questions of balance and compromise that need discussing in advance.

Support

How the staff participate and become involved in work will make a considerable difference to whether the work is a success or not. Staff frequently underestimate their contribution. Not only will commitment and enthusiasm rub off on to the children but it will rub off on to the external partner too.

Recommendations and reports of working with external partners frequently point to the importance of support from senior management. This support ensures that practical commitment to the work is in place along with affirmation of its value and contribution.

TO SUM UP

Urban areas, and rural areas too, are social and cultural patchworks made up of localities with distinctive characteristics and values. Children's centres and schools are increasingly recognising how they work within localities, going out into organisations and centres and to people nearby and inviting them in. This chapter has focused on working with people and places for music within the neighbourhood and on working with visiting musicians who come into the centre. It went on to consider the practical side of projects and setting up working partnerships.

FURTHER READING

Campbell, P. Shehan (2004) *Teaching Music Globally: experiencing music, expressing culture*, Oxford: Oxford University Press.

PART 2

MUSIC WITH CHILDREN

Chapter 5

Listening

A wet, winter's day in London, scaffolding at the windows blocks light and the view. Ten three-year-olds have been indoors all day. Vanessa asks the children to lie on the floor. She puts on a CD and lies down too, alongside the children. The music is a lullaby, played by a small instrumental group with singer. A beautiful horn melody starts. All is calm.

Listening is at the heart of music.

This chapter focuses on listening intently and perceptively, on listening imaginatively and meaningfully, on listening with excitement as the music unfolds, on listening sensitively – and on listening to learn. It will say quite a lot about using recorded music in the Foundation Stage, leaving the individual chapters to introduce listening within the various activities of singing, playing and dancing. Using recorded music, in my view, is a valuable but underused way of creating a rich environment for music. In practical terms, it's a straightforward way to introduce children to a wide variety of interesting music and musical experiences. So I am perplexed as to why it is neglected. The reason is probably because music for young children is so closely associated with singing, with doing music, rather than the full breadth of enriching musical activities.

The ear listens constantly 24/7. We can't close our ears as we can our eyes. It is also, interestingly, the organ for the sense of balance, something we often overlook. Young children can be extra sensitive to sound in a way that we have forgotten. Charlie's ears prick up to small sounds of cracking and creaking in the house or rustles and rumbles out of doors: 'What's that?' he asks, on high alert. The special characteristics of listening

– of really sharp, deep listening, not just hearing – tend to be neglected in education, in spite of it being the bedrock of all learning. So one of the fundamental tasks of education, I think, is to develop in children an alert and conscious listening attention.

SOUNDSCAPES

What kinds of sound environments, 'surround-sound' – a term used by Patricia Campbell (2004) – do the children experience in their classrooms, at home, in their neighbourhood? Are there ever moments of real silence when they can listen with concentration or are their ears jostled by a constant hubbub? What sounds can the children themselves make? Quiet is associated with orderliness and control. Children are expected to learn how to 'be quiet' in their nursery and particularly in school – perhaps at home too – and may be frequently told 'to listen'. It is worth reflecting on what kind of places for sound yourself and the children work in and what is expected of children in terms of being quiet and listening.

A PEDAGOGY OF LISTENING

In early years education there is recent recognition of the importance of listening to children (Clark and Moss, 2001). Listening and taking their ideas and feelings seriously helps to contribute to a sense of respect for their suggestions and efforts, to a sense of calm within the group. It also helps practitioners to understand more precisely what children are doing, thinking, feeling and learning, in music just as in other areas. Thus, 'listening' with its many dimensions – such as adults listening to children's music, children listening intently in all forms of musical activity – blends with this recent practice-wide recognition of the importance of listening to children.

Listening can also be understood as a way of being and living that permeates all practice and relationships within a setting. In the pedagogical theories and practices of the preschools of Reggio Emilia, they have developed what they call 'a pedagogy of listening', by which they mean an openness to others and to the question of meaning. In this very broad sense, listening might expand to include all our senses, to being alert to body movement and sensing it in our own bodies, a kind of empathy beyond the mere act of listening aurally (Young, 1995).

60

I start with listening games – short activities that can be introduced with the explicit purpose of focusing the children's aural attention and creating an atmosphere of quiet and concentrated listening. They are useful preliminaries, not only for music but for any activities where the children will be asked to listen carefully.

LISTENING GAMES

The value of games is that they provide a framework in which a skill can be learned, practised and improved. Games often have a built-in challenge that helps motivate children to participate and practise the skill. Games can also draw in a larger group of children to join in actively.

▶ *What do I have in my box?* A small box with small sound-making objects inside, e.g. some small bells. Take each one out, with ceremony. Listen. Find words to describe the sound.

▶ *Which do you hear?* Play two very similar sounding instruments or two sounds simultaneously. Discriminate between the sounds.

▶ *Do you still hear?* Play an instrument with a sound that fades; or hum and fade the hum. Children close their eyes until the sound fades. Listen with concentration.

▶ *Can you?* Pass a bell or a rattle around a circle without it making a sound and then put it down very quietly. Concentrate, handle the object with dexterity and listen with focus.

▶ *Giant's treasure.* One child guards a collection of jangly metal instruments, eyes closed, and others 'steal' without the giant hearing. Listen with focus. Handle skilfully.

It goes without saying that listening games, if possible, are best played in a stone-dry aural environment where the children can be drawn down into concentrating.

Listening perceptively to music involves:

▶ being attentive;
▶ focusing attention;
▶ picking out something from the whole;
▶ discriminating – telling one sound from another.

61

These processes are followed by describing and by naming, perhaps explaining or thinking about it further, speculating about it or imagining something more. Labelling what is heard can start with the children's vocabulary and then – but cautiously and only when appropriate – move on to conventional terms and vocabulary. In order to develop a genuine understanding of concepts, children need to have had sufficient practical and aural experience.

LISTENING TO RECORDED MUSIC

In everyday life we may listen to recorded music to entertain, to comfort, to change our mood, to liven up some mundane task such as cleaning the house or to keep us company. In the early years settings some of these purposes for listening to recorded music in everyday life will also apply, as well as listening with more explicit educational purposes. The purposes can blend:

- ▶ to create a certain 'feel' for key times of the day – arrival time, resting time, spiritual time;
- ▶ to help along certain activities – clearing up, getting changed;
- ▶ to mark out special occasions such as celebrations or festivals – assembly, an end-of-term party, a festival of light;
- ▶ to entertain – when waiting, when occupied with a meal;
- ▶ to focus on listening – to learn more about the music;
- ▶ to discover new types of music – to hear music from other families, communities, places and times;
- ▶ to accompany another activity – to dance, to sing or play along.

A rich environment for music in the setting will include opportunities for children to listen to a wide variety of music that takes them out and beyond the music they are usually listening to in their home or community life. This is not to imply any value judgement on their home music listening, nor is it a veiled way of saying that children ought to be hearing 'good music' – far from it. It is simply that in most homes (this applies to our homes too), while there could be access to a range of music via radio, TV or the internet, the family is likely to settle into some styles with which they more closely identify. One task of early years education, therefore, is to broaden the children's musical horizons – which usually, incidentally, means broadening our own musical horizons too.

With so much music now available as downloads on subscription sites and the simplicity of MP3 players, it is becoming much easier to build up a listening library of varied music. Equally, CD compilations offer ready-made selections of music from certain times, certain places, certain performers, or associated with a certain mood or purpose. At the end of the chapter are more detailed suggestions for building a listening library.

FREE-CHOICE LISTENING

Access to libraries of music can be made available for children's free-choice listening in much the same way that books are set out to encourage self-guided reading:

> A group of five children in a children's centre in central Bristol were preparing for their carnival day. They were sitting at a computer desk with a range of CDs, some brought in by parents, some belonging to staff, some already part of the nursery resources. They were going through the CDs selecting music that would be suitable for one of their carnival groups to dance to.

At this children's centre the listening area was tucked in a bay to one side. The children had open access to this area and, although the task had been an adult suggestion, the children worked independently, sharing opinions and ideas, making decisions.

Searching for and selecting music

The children can be asked to search and select for certain purposes. Sam in the imaginary day was invited to be the one to select music that day for the drink and snack time. Tasks such as this involve knowing where to look, how to search through CD tracks, imagining what style of music is suitable, and deciding on length, or whether to play a whole track or only part. Younger children would need more assistance; older ones could do this with a high level of independence.

Such activities start children on the road to becoming aware of different styles of music and also how music fits certain activities, occasions and moods. With older children, choices can be discussed in whole-group times, with the selection reduced to a few options that are then listened to and discussed for appropriateness.

PASSIVE AND ACTIVE LISTENING

A distinction is sometimes made between passive and active listening. As suggested by the terms, passive refers to music that is on in the background and where the child is not obviously engaged. That said, it is difficult to make a clear-cut distinction. Children may be sitting in the entrance hall, waiting; music is playing, and they are listening very intently. Equally, they may be dancing wildly but are more wrapped up in their movement than paying attention to the music.

While eating a snack or meal is a good time for indirect listening and this can then spark interest in the music:

> One small combined nursery and reception class in a rural Forest of Dean school put recorded music on to play while the children were sitting quietly around tables having their drink and fruit. They found that it created a relaxed moment, particularly if they chose quieter music at a slower tempo. During this time the children would comment on the music – 'that sounds like ballet music' or 'that's music like my Dad has'. The teacher listened in and noted some of these comments. She also added her own. Sometimes these focused on the style of music, or on the people who played the music, but mostly she added comments in terms of the music's qualities, to model ways of describing music.

As a general rule, however, young children find it difficult to just sit and listen without somehow being actively involved, usually moving in some way. The sections that follow suggest various ways in which the children might participate in music as it plays. The exception may be if they are listening to a live performance and the fascination of watching the players holds their attention. When Michael played his violin, as I described in the previous chapter, he attracted an audience of children who barely moved an inch for a long period of time. Children experiencing a live performance may sit stock still for relatively long periods.

LEARNING TO BE A LISTENER

For adults to model attentive, active listening is the first key way to encourage the children to listen attentively too. Body language and eye contact will show involvement. Music education advice often recommends that this would include not talking, if possible, while the music plays. But, on the contrary, I have found that certain small prompters or descriptive comments, such as 'oh, what loud trumpets' or 'shhh, this is a very, very quiet bit', can help to support the children's listening and involvement – a form of structured interaction.

Moving to the music

To move and dance to live and recorded music is a valuable and vivid experience for children. Indeed, to stay still is impossible with some music – the impulse to move is irresistible. It can range from children joining in with simple dance moves that are prescribed by a communal dance form – a folk dance, children's ring game or warm-up disco routine – to dancing freely, as the imagination takes them. In the chapter on dancing I pick up and develop these ideas.

Wendy Sims experimented with young children's listening to recorded music when they were just listening, or listening while also being active in movement. She found that active listening tended to encourage children to listen for longer, that they were more attentive and that they could remember more about the music afterwards (Sims, 1986). So it would appear, on the basis of research evidence, that moving to music can be particularly worthwhile in terms of children's learning.

Singing to the music

Singing along to recorded versions of songs may offer an approach to some early childhood professionals who feel less competent at leading song-singing without the back-up of a recording. One word of caution: producers of these recordings of songs for children have rarely heeded the available information on children's developing voices. All too often, in producing something that sounds bright and breezy, recorded versions of children's songs zip along at too fast a pace, at too high a pitch and with complicated words. Trying to manage words, melody and often actions as well can be a frustrating experience for children. However, there *are* some CDs that are well suited for children to sing with, mainly produced by educational publishers, and, used judiciously, these can provide models and interesting instrumental accompaniments. Moreover, these CDs can be made available for children to use in developing their own singing activities, in free play or in adult-structured, but independent activities.

Finding recordings with interesting examples of singers for children to listen to, to imitate and explore how differently voices can be used, is a valuable and enjoyable activity. Children will appreciate the resonant virtuosity of operatic singers, the smooch of jazz singers, the nasal earthiness of some folk singers, the amazing variety of vocal styles found in musics from around the world. Again, these can either be provided as part of a free-choice listening selection or be developed in guided listening sessions.

Children may pick out different vocal techniques – elaborate trills and ornaments of an operatic singer, the scat singing of jazz, a wobbly vibrato or very clear, high-pitched sound. They enjoy trying to imitate these vocal styles – and indeed should have the opportunity to try, either while the CD is playing or after. Sitting in hushed, reverent silence is not necessary. Children using their voices in interesting ways outside the normal boundaries of voice use in nursery or school seems to arouse anxiety in educators. Partly I think this is due to the enormous reticence in our own society about using the voice; we are shy voice users. Partly, too, it is due to anxiety about control. A class of children warbling with Pavarotti may raise some eyebrows, but what joy!

Playing to the music

We all know the fun of playing 'air guitar'. It is a way of getting inside the music. When we watch players live or on screen, part of the experience is to imagine what it must feel like, to identify with the physical act of making that music. Video recordings of musicians playing are increasingly available, and musicians from the locality, traditional music groups, orchestras or family members can be encouraged to visit – as indeed I was suggesting in the chapters on musical childhoods and neighbourhoods. If possible, make a recording of their visit so that the children can listen (and watch) again later.

One of the responses children often show spontaneously when listening to live music is to imitate the actions of playing. Encouraging this and describing how the instrument is played builds on from this response:

Patrick Harrild brought his huge, bright shiny tuba into the nursery. The sound was fat and round, filling the room. It could be mellow, it could bellow, thrilling the children with every note. They contorted their lips and mouth positions in imitation and curved out their arms to hug imaginary tubas, fingers working imaginary valves.

Joining in a live performance

For the children to play instruments that actually make a sound along with the recording or live performance may sound like a recipe for chaos. There are quite a number of CDs intended for educational purposes that encourage playing along with some light percussion instruments or drums. One browsing session took me to several websites where these are available. I found exciting reggaes, raps, folk-style pieces and contemporary rock, all written for children but interesting music in its own right. It's worth reflecting, for a moment, that, just as there are excellent books written just for children, there is increasingly music being thoughtfully composed for children's listening and joining in.

When children have a chance to play the piano or set out some drums like a drum kit, they often act out playing the instrument, drawing on models of musical performance that they have seen and heard. Michael, the violinist we heard about in Chapter 4, had played some virtuosic gypsy music, 'scrubbing' his bow rapidly to and fro to produce trembling sounds. A week later he brought in a child-size violin and bow. The children could imitate his actions and, by playing alongside them, Michael gave them an experience of enacting the music, of being 'inside' it with them.

> Nancy Evans is a trumpeter. She brought in a saxoflute set from which the children could construct all kinds of differently shaped, differently sounding trumpet-like instruments. As she performed, moving around the outdoor area, so the children marched along with her, toot-tooting.

Making the music

Once Michael had left the nursery, he loaned his child-size violin so that the children could play their own 'gypsy music' during the week. What actually sounded out might have seemed like disconnected, scratchy sounds, but in the children's imaginations they were being Michael playing the music. The staff in the nursery knew the background to the children's playing and could recognise in their activity how they were creating – and re-creating – their own versions. And creating music does not mean that it has to be entirely original; indeed, musical ideas always come from somewhere. When Vijay and Sam were playing drums in the description of the imaginary nursery at the very start of this book, they were drawing on models of playing they had witnessed.

Certain styles of music may lend themselves more to this kind of activity, such as those for solo instrument or with a distinctive playing style. Here are some suggestions as starting points:

- ▶ bhangra music – dhol drum;
- ▶ Evelyn Glennie – percussionist, whose CDs often include music played on very simple percussion instruments;
- ▶ Japanese Shakuhachi music – a solo, bamboo flute melody that meanders;
- ▶ Spanish flamenco music – strumming on a guitar.

In these kinds of approaches, the children are absorbing whatever features of the music strike them and they are drawn to. When they re-create, it is those features that they rework in some way. When the children tooted on saxoflutes with Nancy playing a Haydn trumpet concerto, they were listening with careful attention to her playing and joining in with it, picking up certain things, such as the way she held the instrument and aspects of rhythm and timbre.

FOCUSED LISTENING

Having described first of all more experiential, self-directed activities involving recorded music, it is equally valuable to structure activities, to prompt and scaffold the children's listening. There may be some characteristic of the music that is valuable to pick up and emphasise in movement, in singing with it or playing so that the children become more aware of it. They may be asked to move in a way that matches characteristics of time and duration; to listen for the beat of the music and step it out or sway to and fro in time. They may listen out for certain rhythmic ideas that occur every now and then and join in by tapping along with instruments. They may sing along in a way that picks up some aspect of the pitch – a melody that sits on a single note for a long time, or that falls step by step or that undulates gently. The advantage of such activities is that the children's response to what they hear can be immediate and direct, and all are actively participating. By converting their responses into a musical medium – singing, moving, playing – the children do not need verbal labels to demonstrate they have heard and understood.

Listen for and move

Vanessa King, working in Islington nurseries and schools, uses a repertoire of activities performed to recorded music that encourage the children to focus on certain musical features. In one example, she structured the activity, building it step by step. First, she asked the children to plod from foot to foot, heavy-footed, then to practise the movement on the spot. Next, she played music with a slow, heavy beat, asking them to listen first, then gradually join in, making their steps fit with the music. She watched all the children, noticing those who were less successful at matching stepping tempo to music tempo and giving extra support where needed.

Vanessa planned for repeat listenings not only within a session, but also week on week. The repeat listenings varied the ways in which the children were engaged, so that different aspects of the music could slip in and out of focus. She skilfully ratcheted up the challenge too, usually by withdrawing her prompts and assistance.

Listen for and sing

Penny, a student teacher working in a Devon reception class, played the children a piece of folk music based on a drone – a single, continuous pitched sound that sounded through the whole piece. She asked the children to listen for the drone note (altering the balance on the CD player so that it was more prominent). She hummed it to draw attention to it and then asked the children to hum it with her.

In many curricula for young children, the musical elements are separated out into rhythm, tempo (fast and slow), melody, pitch and dynamics (loud and soft), and texture and timbre as if these are objective 'things' in the music that can be picked out, isolated, understood and then recognised when they occur in other music.

The first difficulty is that in music all these elements work together and interact with one another. As in cooking, it is not the individual ingredients but their combination that makes the dish delicious. We might well comment on one ingredient – or element – but also need to think how it works in combination with others. An energetically exciting piece of jazz music may have a melody that moves very quickly over many different pitches, with rapid rhythmic activity and lots of instruments playing together in a thick, rough texture.

Inviting children to say what they heard in the music and to use their own vocabulary is valuable. Children can respond to and understand musical characteristics and concepts before they can use the precise terminology themselves. First, they need to hear the vocabulary, modelled for them, before they can use it independently. So for adults to describe the music, to say what is happening, is an important early stage. All too often adults question children rather than talk to them about music or develop 'thematic conversations' as they were termed by the EPPE Project team.

RESOURCES

The quality of the sound of recorded music will be greatly improved by good equipment – particularly the size of speakers. So often in early years settings I spot a small, battered portable CD player sitting on a desk or windowsill. The tiny inbuilt speakers are not designed for larger spaces. MP3 players have the advantage that they can either be listened to individually with headphones, by small groups using a splitter and headphones, or connected to good-quality speakers for whole-room and larger-group listening.

Music for listening

Music for listening in early years settings is often confined to a narrow diet of light classics or commercially produced music for children, typically nursery rhyme compilations. While there may be a small amount of music that is best avoided because of unsuitable lyrics, there need be no other boundaries around music for children to listen to. The simple checklist below will help the process of building up a varied music collection and will prompt the search and select process. The music might cover a range of:

- ▶ *times* – a very long time ago (medieval troubadour music), quite a long time ago (romantic piano music), recent (contemporary film music);
- ▶ *places* – far away (American first-nation songs), not so far away (Greek folk dance), local;
- ▶ *styles* – familiar styles (brass band), less familiar styles (Brazilian carnival music), very unfamiliar styles (Chinese opera);
- ▶ *purposes* – film music, religious music, lullabies;
- ▶ *instrument types* – blown, percussion, stringed – and singers;

▶ groups – very large groups (orchestra, full choir), largish groups (jazz group, drumming ensemble), small groups or solo.

What follows is not intended to be a prescriptive or definitive list, but merely to give some starting suggestions to setting up a library of CDs and DVDs or a playlist. One of the most useful series I have found are the compilation CDs produced by Rough Guide. They not only offer many compilations of world, jazz, folk and pop music, their list includes various compilations of children's music such as *Reggae Playground* and *Latin Music for Children*.

Instruments

▶ Early English instruments: English Cornett and Sackbut Ensemble.
▶ Brass band: Grimethorpe Colliery, *Brass Band Classics*.
▶ Spanish guitar: Paco Peña, *The Art of Paco Peña*.
▶ Ghanaian instruments: Ewe drumming.
▶ Electric guitar: Eric Clapton.
▶ Classical piano: Chopin ballades.
▶ Sitar: northern Indian classical music.

Singers and voices

▶ Sarah Brightman.
▶ Ladysmith Black Mambazo.
▶ Dolly Parton.
▶ Welsh male voice choirs.
▶ Bulgarian women's groups.
▶ The Three Tenors.

Music and dance

▶ Stomp (videos of dance and percussion using everyday items).
▶ Bollywood films.
▶ Classical ballet: the male *Swan Lake*.
▶ Traditional Irish folk dances.

Music and film

There are many possibilities here:

▶ John Williams: tracks for *Harry Potter* films.

FURTHER READING

Clark, A. and Moss, P. (2001) *Listening to Young Children: the mosaic approach*, London: National Children's Bureau.

Young, S. and Glover, J. (1998) *Music in the Early Years*, London: The Falmer Press.

Chapter 6

Voices

An area of floor was spread with a watery-blue cloth and on it Ann had laid out plastic sea creatures of all kinds, including jellyfish, some wooden blocks to be 'rocks' and fishing nets. She sat on the floor in this area and, when children arrived who were interested to play, she sang a song while they acted out its sequence of jumping jellyfish. In one play episode, Jake sang only one part of the song, but sang this repeatedly with a deep, wobbly voice on the word 'jellyfish'. He obviously enjoyed doing this as he repeated it several times. At the same time he clutched a plastic jellyfish, which he wobbled on a rock as he sang and then flung into the blue cloth sea. Two girls joined in the play. They sat on Ann's knee being the jellyfish themselves. Ann 'wobbled' them on her knee and they laughed, enjoying the warm, one-to-one contact with an adult they knew well. Acting out the jellyfish song, they jumped off Ann's knee and into the sea, singing as they did so. They then played with the fishing nets and Ann watched and listened as they continued to sing not only bits of this song, but also to make up a new melody to similar words. Finally, they 'caught' Ann in a fishing net by popping it on her head. Everyone laughed.

Within all this activity the song was sung, in snatches, with added vocalisations, with interesting voices. It was sung in full and sung with transformations and variations to fit with the children's activity. The children improvised their play with and around the song, with and around the things, and with and around Ann. They went on not only to reproduce the song, singing independently, but also to create a new song.

I suggest that this kind of song-play activity allows the children to be more autonomous and creative in their song-singing than is the case during the more usual kind of adult-guided song-singing sessions. What's more,

73

the songs were repeated several times over, either by Ann to accompany the children's play or to support their own singing, or by the children in solo singing. The songs were sung slowly and deliberately in ways that fitted with how the children were leading the singing themselves and gave them ample opportunity to 'get on board' with the song. Songs performed by adults in group sessions are frequently sung too quickly for young children, particularly if taken from commercial recordings. Ann sometimes prompted a child's singing by starting and then withdrawing her own voice, or sometimes lightly joined in when the child's singing faltered. Importantly, her contributions were not leading but were contingent and responsive to how the children were singing. She watched and listened and tailored her input accordingly. Having someone who takes special interest in listening to you sing is a real boost.

The development of these song-play activities as one of a set of free-choice options evolved from reflective discussions with all the staff in this children's centre about ways to line up music, song-singing in this case, with the more general, play-based principles that underpinned other areas of the curriculum.

Significantly, the several repetitions of the same song at slow speeds and opportunity for individual practice, which are ingredients for successful learning of songs and the development of song-singing skills, were automatically built into the song-play activities. These are approaches advocated by music education pedagogy and are rarely included in the usual group song-singing sessions. I am not suggesting that this kind of song-play activity replaces larger group communal song-singing sessions, but that careful thought is given to the purpose of singing activities, to how they are carried out and to what children are learning and gaining.

In this nursery, staff went on to became inventive at incorporating songs into all kinds of ongoing activities: I heard a little ditty made up between adult and child about going to hang up her coat; I heard an improvised song included for outdoor play on bikes that reminded children to stay within some lines; I heard a made-up song for children playing with small figures at a castle.

SINGING

Singing is the mainstay of musical activity with children in nurseries and schools, so much so that it is frequently taken for granted. Almost every group or class has a regular daily short session when all come together to sing through some favourite repertoire. It is so commonplace that it may be rare to stop and question the 'whys and hows' of this activity.

Singing songs can bring a group of children together – it is a truly communal activity, and if I start to ask some more searching questions about group song-singing, it is not to downplay its value as a sociable activity. I have seen 80 nursery and reception children gathered together on the final day of a summer term for a sing-song with accompanying musician on accordion, which was uplifting for children, staff and parents and gave a real sense of occasion to mark this special time. But, equally, I have seen children cross-legged on the carpet being urged to sit still while a few well-worn songs are sung through in routine fashion with no musical sparkle.

There are three principles to hold in mind:

▶ *Children learn to sing* – it is not something some can do and some can't, or just something that you pick up; it is 'learnable' and so teachable too.
▶ *Selecting appropriate songs is important* – for learning singers this is key to their success.
▶ *Children are inventive singers* – they can improvise and make up their own songs.

LEARNING TO BE A SINGER

As with any aspect of development, it is impossible to map out a universal, simple pathway that all children would progress along. A huge amount depends on the nature of their experiences in their years at home since birth. Some musical childhoods will be singing-rich, with lots of songs from TV or radio, and with adults who sing along for their own pleasure and expect the young children to take pleasure in songs too. These parents and carers are likely to sing to and with their children and include song-singing as a natural and easy part of everyday family life. In interviewing parents about their home music activities with children we heard about little special, quiet songs for bedtime, quite often linked to the family religion, or spiritual in some other way, or a song that always has to be sung on a bus journey, or songs to be sung in the car, or a silly song for walking along the road. These songs are woven into everyday life, and often contribute to parenting strategies. Equally, there were some families for whom music was less important, perhaps for religious reasons or because they have fewer resources for playing music, or it's just not something these families did. So children come into early education with varying prior experiences of being sung to and being encouraged to participate. Becoming a singer is not just about learning to use the voice and remember tunes and words; it also includes self-identity as a member of a family, community or school where music makes an active contribution.

POSSIBLE PATTERNS OF DEVELOPMENT

Given that children have a wide range of background experiences, there are some likely patterns of development to look out for. It's useful to separate out what children do when they are joining in with performed songs, and when they are singing their own made-up songs, spontaneously.

Graham Welch (2006) has spent years studying children's singing development and how they learn to sing. He has arrived at the following four phases. He does not suggest that these rigidly apply to all children, nor does he suggest that they apply in all contexts. But as I mentioned when talking about interpreting observations, such frameworks are useful in helping us to understand the processes by which children learn to sing 'in tune' (and even here, 'in tune' may mean different things in different musical traditions), in helping us to understand children's singing and in helping us to decide how best to help them.

> ► *Phase 1* The words are the centre of interest, rather than the melody. Singing is often described as 'chant-like', the range of pitches is limited and the phrases are melodically simple.
>
>   Think of a children's chant, for example, 'See-saw Marjorie Daw' or 'It's Raining, It's Pouring'. These sit on just two or three pitches. Explore how children sing these songs. Invite children to sing them on their own and listen carefully.

> ► *Phase 2* There is growing awareness that changing vocal pitch is a conscious process and controllable. The children now can sing more approximately according to the melody of the song, perhaps generally following the overall up and down, melodic contours of the song or matching one or two key parts – often, say, a chorus that is catchy and repeats. The range of pitches they use begins to expand.

Take a simple song you are confident the children know. 'The Wheels on the Bus' is a good example. Listen out for the last phrase 'all day long'. Most children will have heard that the word 'day' is at a lower pitch than its two neighbours. Listen to how the children sing that final phrase in particular, and then, in addition, to how they manage the first phrase.

▶ *Phase 3* The children can sing a song, providing it is not too complex, mostly accurately. They might shift tonality – that means, a section of a song sounds alright in itself, but it didn't quite follow on in the right key from the previous section.

Take another very familiar song, 'Twinkle, Twinkle Little Star'. Sing it to yourself and focus on the second phrase 'How I wonder what you are'. Now notice how the next phrase, 'Up above the world so high' comes down, step by step, in exactly the same shape, but a note higher. The third phrase does the same. Then the very last 'How I wonder what you are' has shifted down again. How do the children sing it? Probably they can sing the downward phrases step by step, but the starting note may shift about.

▶ *Phase 4* Children can sing relatively simple songs that are from a familiar repertoire with pitch and rhythmic accuracy.

Graham Welch developed this understanding from a large study of children in a number of London schools who were just starting out in reception classes. Most interestingly, in one school, as they tracked children over the next three years, all the children made progress in their singing. This was a school serving an area of low socio-economic status and low academic achievement in other areas of the curriculum. In contrast, in another school serving those of higher socio-economic status and attainment levels, the children made no progress. The difference was in teacher expectation. The first teacher had high expectations, and she worked consistently with all the pupils over a sustained period. One teacher, in one school, for one year can make a big and lasting difference (Welch, 2006).

Most importantly, he points out that children will be at different levels of singing ability when they arrive in the early years of nursery and schooling. But this does not mean that those children in the earlier phases of singing cannot learn to sing, particularly if given the right opportunities: 'a nurturing environment in which singing tasks are designed to match, then extend, current vocal behaviours' (Welch, 2006: 319).

First, children learn by being able to listen to models of singing, either live from the adults around them, from other children or from recordings. Second, they need to be provided with opportunities to sing that are at just the right level of challenge. Third, they improve by being able to listen to themselves sing and receiving encouragement, feedback and well-tailored assistance.

Providing models of singing overlaps with ideas already discussed in relation to listening and working with live performers. But it is also about adults within the setting singing to and for the children, as Ann did. For some adults, this can arouse deep-set memories of hurt and injustice when they were told as children that they could not sing.

In current practice, those who work with young children are aware that thoughtless negative comments can seep deeply into feelings and identity. However, putting down one's own singing ability or other people's singing is part of English culture. Here is an anecdote from my own experiences. At a recent general early years education conference, one speaker didn't appear for a small seminar and so the chair jokingly asked for a stand-in to do a 'song and dance' act. To which I, equally jokingly, sang a bit of a pop song. 'Oh, stop! no more of that, we'll call you, don't call us!' I was laughingly told. This was not a reflection of *how* I sang, but just the acceptable, general repartee that circulates in our culture about singing. Here, in a general early years conference, these professionals, full of thoughtful, expert ideas within their own spheres of practice, still held on to some unconsidered views – clichés – about singing. So, although we know better than to voice negative comments to children about singing, the deep-set ideas still influence how singing is thought about in current practice.

JOINING IN WITH PERFORMED SONGS

Selecting songs to suit children's current ability levels is important so that the song presents them with just the right level of challenge. Singing melodically simpler songs is obviously more achievable than singing long, complex songs. Take the most popular song of all – 'Twinkle, Twinkle Little Star'. It starts with repeated and simple words. It follows a clear melody line with no complex rhythms. Most people sing it quite slowly and deliberately. But compare this with another early years favourite, 'Five Currant Buns in a Baker's Shop'. Here the song is much longer and more complex, the melody twists and turns around many different pitches and the words are confusingly split over two or more pitches ('ba – ker's' and 'su – gar'). This poses a much greater singing challenge. If the purpose of an activity is to assist children in their singing skills, the song selection is key. It is not that singing activities need to be restricted to learnable songs, but only that the song should suit the purpose.

So what characteristics make songs more accessible for early singers? These are:

- a limited pitch range;
- a descending melody shape;
- short clear phrases;
- a slower pace;
- rhythms that are not too complex.

So it stands to reason that providing songs for children to sing that fit these characteristics will help children to get on board with singing. With more complex songs, some children may well still manage to learn to sing successfully, but it is likely that a significant band of children will get lost and start to fall behind. A simple parallel with learning to read is useful here. Some children will learn with ease, while others will need carefully planned and structured input in order to develop their skills.

The voice has different registers – low, middle and high. The lowest register is commonly used for speaking and is the register that many young children at first use for singing – hence, for some, the difficulty in distinguishing between singing and speaking voice. In terms of pitch range, researchers have explored in careful detail just what range suits young voices, remembering that the vocal folds are softer and shorter than those of mature voices, and the lung capacity is smaller (Rutkowski and Runfola, 2007). The consensus of opinion is that, as a guideline, songs should range between the D just above middle C to the B, a range of just six notes: a small range. This tends to be lower than many published songs are pitched, but higher than adult women singers often pitch their voices. Alison Harmer working in Gloucestershire recommends taking one of the small, single octave C-C glockenspiels that are frequently found among early childhood percussion equipment and, finding the D-B pitch range, using this as a quick guide for getting a sense of children's pitch range. Going back to our two sample songs, 'Twinkle, Twinkle' sits on the six-note range, whereas 'Currant Buns' wanders far outside it. Indeed, so do many of the favourite nursery songs. This would explain why so many children have difficulty singing them. The songs are just not very singable for three- to five-year-old voices. Find the right song, at the right pitch, and children have much more chance of singing successfully.

Feedback

You can see how therefore, if the ability to sing is believed to be in the genes and not learnable, there is little need to think carefully how singing is provided for, to plan, observe, record and so on, nor to give any specific feedback. Hence the tendency in early childhood settings to praise children's singing enthusiastically, irrespective of how they have sung. To apply rigour and to challenge children to strive to do better – when I suggest this to practitioners – is frequently thought to be overly harsh. But if we understand singing to be something children learn how to do, and that education has a responsibility to help them in learning, then giving feedback to help children improve is a key part of that process.

Some approaches to supporting children's singing development recommend that children be given opportunities to sing alone because then they can listen to their own voices. Certainly, in the full sound of a school assembly it is difficult for children to be aware of how they are singing themselves. And certainly too, to be able to hear yourself and monitor what you are doing is important. Many children are encouraged to sing at home, and will do so on their own, setting their own pitch, pace and so on. It's not the risky task we adults sometimes imagine for children to sing solo. For a very few, it may be terrifying. You will know your own children and judge. Songs, particularly singing games, where children take a turn to sing alone for short turns, are useful for this reason.

Focusing on detail

More formal song-performing or song-listening activities provide good opportunities to focus children's attention on musical detail. 'At the beginning of the song, the tune jumps up and then it comes down by step – listen to me sing it again.' In Chapter 9 I will go into more detail about how this kind of learning focus can be developed. The learning spotlight might be shone on a rhythmic detail, perhaps picking out a short section of the song words and chanting, then tapping, then moving these to draw attention to, to make conscious and to practise the rhythmic patterning.

This kind of learning detail, focusing on units of pitch, or rhythm, or dynamics, is quite conventional in music education practice and curriculum materials can provide plenty of ideas. There are two points to add. One is to be cautious that these learning activities do not become an end in themselves. It's as if the zoom lens focuses in on some musical detail, and then back out again to the whole musical experience. The second is to include musical detail such as timbre, or the way the voice is used, or the kind of dance and performance style that is associated, say, with a video of singing, particularly with four- going on five-year-olds. Just focusing on pitch or rhythm is only one tiny strand (and often not the most interesting strand to be honest) of the kind of musical detail that makes singing come alive. I doubt the amateur singers being coached on TV singing competitions are being asked to clap rhythm patterns, but they are focused on the detail of how to create a certain vocal tone, how to twist or turn the melody to make it more expressive, how to fade at the end of a phrase, how to inflect their voices – all the expressive things that we recognise as essentially musical, but are so difficult to put your finger on.

In 'singing simple songs from memory', as the Foundation Stage requires, it is important to be clear that learning and remembering the melody and the words of a song are two different tasks. Learning a set of words is a language task more than a musical task. Working with some four-year-olds, Taka, newly arrived from Japan, was clearly able to sing along with the songs, pitching his voice accurately for the most part, joining in with the others with confidence and enthusiasm. But when I listened in, he sang to odd vowel and consonant sounds that he'd picked up from my singing. I would count this as being able to sing a simple song from memory even though he was not singing the actual words.

And when you start to think about it in more detail, there are more complications. We might need to think, as well, about whether the children are singing:

- the whole song or just parts of the song – typically the chorus or some catch lines that stand out;
- the melody accurately or with some variation;
- on their own, with a partner or small group, or with the whole group;

► with an accompaniment and, if so, what kind of accompaniment – a quiet guitar strumming a few chords may give a very subtle support, while a karaoke-style backing track on CD may be so rich and full that the singing voice is almost lost.

SPONTANEOUS SINGING

Young children use their voices, some almost continuously, in a wide range of expressive, inventive forms of playful singing – or it might be better to call these 'vocalisations' since many of these forms of playful voice use blur the boundaries between speech, singing and making voice sounds (Young, 2002). This rich seam of creative, playful activity is going on all the time under our noses in early years settings and yet it rarely gets noticed, let alone commented on, encouraged or extended (Young, 2006). All too often children's creative music activity is confined to play with instruments rather than singing or even singing-drama. Read through the curriculum documents and you will see that, subtly, the expectation is that singing will be mainly a reproductive activity (sing some known songs) and the creative, imaginative activity will be with musical instruments. There are some mentions of spontaneous vocalisations, but more as a response among the younger children than as a creative activity.

LIKELY PATTERNS OF INTEREST

I carried out some studies of young children's spontaneous vocalisations (Young, 2002, 2006). From these observations I have suggested some recurring types of singing play, grouping these into different types. I write about these here to suggest some starting points for your own observation and interpretation. There are, as well, some other valuable and important studies of children's singing play (Marsh and Young, 2006; Sundin, 1998).

A musical drama

Here is a role play, an 'opera scene' between two boys, observed in the same London nursery where Ann was working:

'Come on? Do you want to have your supper?' chants Jack to Joel. The chanting sits on one pitch then falls characteristically on the final syllable of 'supper'. Joel stamps across the room intoning the same question to match his stomps and concludes the phrase by jumping on the spot emphatically on the word 'supper'.

'Come back here! Come back here!' sings Joel repeatedly to Jack as he runs after him. Joel sings on a two-note melody that moves up a step and back. A game of chasing ensues, but the 'Come back here!' melody is woven into their various chasings and runnings.

The game is more a make-believe chase than a real attempt at escape and capture – a kind of pantomime chase – for the boys both run randomly in all directions and both chant 'Come back here!'

They then return to the play house, but one chants rhythmically on a falling perfect 4th* 'Get the boat, get the boat, get the boat Joel!' and repeats the same phrase two more times with matching pace and rhythm.

A sudden call of 'We're drowning!' prompts both boys to fall to the floor and flail about calling out 'We're drowning! We're drowning!' This then changes quite suddenly to 'Joel, help us! Joel, help us!' see-sawing clearly on the same interval of a falling perfect 4th. The heightened drama leads to a new suggestion of 'We need emergency'. This is not clearly pitched but declaimed slowly with rhythmic emphasis on each of the vowels of e – merg – en – cy.

Help is at hand. Both boys, in an instant role change, become the Thunderbirds who fly in singing their theme tune with many fff, shshs sounds as they come into land, arms outstretched. An imaginary rescue is acted out, which they manage to complete while nursery staff urge the boys to contribute to 'tidy up' time. In a clever compromise between their own desire to finish the action and not ignore the request, the play house stuff is 'rescued' and put back by the Thunderbirds still singing.

The TV *Thunderbirds* cartoon carries vivid images of sound and movement. This TV theme tune (brought into their nursery play from home) is full of energy and strength that the children could draw into

---

*The interval of a perfect 4th is the first interval of 'Away in a Manger'. Sing 'away' to yourself and you hear a 4th; now sing 'way, away, away, away' to yourself and you have Joel's melody.

themselves by singing it. Their theme of 'danger-rescue' is a recurring theme in children's role play. The boys' many forms of singing provide the functions of singing in musical drama – to announce, provoke or achieve a change in the direction of the action, to emphasise an action and express a heightened state of emotion. Their singing is closely entwined with their narrative action.

Playing with known songs

Songs that the children already know, either from their experiences of multimedia or from Foundation Stage settings, reappear, perhaps in short, remembered snatches, perhaps in longer sections, often with altered melodies and words. We saw the two girls do this with the jellyfish song at the start of this chapter.

This repetitive singing of short sections, or altered melodies, may arise because the children do not yet remember the song exactly, or their vocal range and voice technique are not yet developed enough to manage the full pitch range. Sometimes, however, I think children have no need to sing the complete song from beginning to end. Certainly with some three- and four-year-olds, I have been struck by how they are often able to sing a song they know well from beginning through to end if I asked them to, but in their play they rarely did so. It is, after all, much more fun, more interesting, to play with the song, to fit it around what you are doing at the moment, make it match a movement, make the words fit the toy you have, to add some melody of your own making. When we have a song 'on the brain', we rarely sing the whole thing, but a phrase or two that has really got a hold. It surfaces in association with what we are doing, in variations of our own making.

Free melody

Listen to children singing of their own volition and they are not only using song melodies of known songs but also improvising their own melodies. There seem to be two main types of self-made melody. One type consists of long, freely meandering threads of melody on open vowel sounds. It typically occurs during focused play, when children are playing alone and often with small objects and toys requiring concentration. The following is a typical example:

Callum was threading beads on a lace and, as he did so, he sung to himself with a fluid, free-floating melody on an open syllable sound 'aah!' When two beads were threaded he altered his melody to short dipping phrases to match the beads swinging to and fro on the lace.

Just as mothers sing to babies to help calm and soothe, so I have the idea that young children can sing themselves down into a state of physical calmness required for mental focus. Again, as adults we often use music to help regulate our physical and emotional state in much the same kind of way.

Chant

Another type of melody I noted in my study was typically a short melodic idea or phrase, with a rhythmic pattern that children would repeat over and over again. Frequently these types of melodic chant were sung to significant words or short phrases, again fitting closely with their play:

Kasha was playing at the water tray and had tipped a plastic figure out of a small boat into the water. As it bobbed about, she dipped her hand in to paddle the figure along and sang 'swim, swim, swim', in a regular grouping of three. Each group sat on three regular beats with a pause between and the pitches were clear, the middle 'swim' being sung a note higher than its two neighbours.

Interestingly, her singing was almost imperceptible, but that day we were filming in the nursery for a video on children's musical activity and the sound recordist's sensitive equipment had picked up her song. I thought I was quite good at hearing young children's singing, but I missed this completely! It goes to show how easy it is to become complacent that we are hearing and seeing young children and how we must continually struggle to remain alert.

Movement singing

Children's vocalisations were also fused with movement – either their own physical movement or the movement of the things they were playing with. We saw how Callum's bead-threading song changed as the beads swung to and fro, his vocalisations changing to match the swing. Similarly,

85

there were many instances of children singing their movements. It is as if they are wired up on all systems and physical energy and exuberance is also expressed in vocalisations. One interesting example illustrates the close integration of the movement of toys and self-movement:

> Ben was lobbing a little cloth doll about two metres into the air so that it arced just ahead of him and fell to the floor. As he lobbed he chanted 'up the choo' (this is how I heard it) and the 'choo' matched the doll's flight – elongated and curved in his voice. The 'up the' he sang as he held the doll in both hands readying to throw. Having lobbed the doll three times, he then took a couple of steps, saying 'up the' as he did so and jumped himself into the air with the 'choo'.

The transfer of doll movement to his own movement seemed to pivot on his rhythmic, contoured, verbal chant. To transform an activity into vocalisation converts it into a very flexible form. It gives the child a kind of 'grip' on an experience as it emphasises certain aspects of how the movement is structured – its timing is a translation of flight in space, its contour a translation of the curve of the throw – but a very flexible grip that helps to support a quick conversion of the time-space idea into self-movement.

Singing for toys

Children often vocalise vehicles, animals and people to bring them to life in their play, often giving them voice-markers – gruff animal sounds, sirens, engine sounds and so on:

> Leah makes a descending string of 'chuc, chuc, chuc' sounds for rotating blades as she flies the helicopter in to land. But a moment later, when she grips the paramedic, she makes the same singing sound to indicate that he needs to fly off again.

The helicopter 'song' (perhaps it is a wild exaggeration to call it a song, but I think sometimes stretching concepts helps in the process of rethinking) is now detached from the flying movement and is representative of that toy, indicating the next move in her game.

SONG-MAKING IN GROUP ACTIVITY

When working with a group of children, improvised vocalising and making up songs can be introduced as more structured activities, initiated by the adult. These can draw on all of the children's spontaneous song-making strategies that I have discussed above. The children might be invited to play around with known songs, inventing new versions, to sing stories for toys, to sing while they move, to make free melodies like scat singing, to chant or to make up call-and-response songs.

Coral Davies made a study of children's invented songs, of which she collected numerous samples (Davies, 1992). She led the children in a singing session and then simply asked if someone would like to make up a song. As the children became accustomed to this activity, so the more they willingly improvised songs on the spot. One of the things to learn from this is that what we expect from children is what we get.

Liz Terry, working as an early years voice specialist across Gloucestershire, joined an outing to a forest environment. The children sang songs about digging up worms and snails; they sat in a line making up a song about 'driving an aeroplane'. Liz's role was first and foremost to listen, to prompt, or to join in if she thought this would help – structuring her interactions as she judged would best help the children to invent their songs. Thus she adopted the pedagogical role of structured interaction – one of the main themes of this book – taking the children's starting points and judging how to add to them to construct little ditties and songs.

TO SUM UP

This chapter has discussed children using their voices in some detail, both in how they learn to sing ready-made songs or how they sing inventively and creatively in their own play. Singing is the mainstay of early years music and yet this area, too, would benefit from expanded repertoires of practice, moving on from the simple reproduction of familiar songs to work that uses singing creatively and inventively, to work that is well designed and tailored to developing children's skills as singers and, harking back to the listening chapter, to work that expands their understanding of singing styles and cultures, including popular culture. And singing work that links with worlds outside – of family, neighbourhood and afar, and the intersections of all of these.

FURTHER READING

Davies, C. (1992) '"Listen to my song": a study of songs invented by children aged from 5 to 7 years', *British Journal of Music Education* 9(1): 19–48.

Rutkowski, J. and Runfola, M. (eds) (1997; 2nd edn) *Tips: the child voice*, Lanham, MA: Rowman and Littlefield Publishers.

Young, S. (2006) 'Seen but not heard: young children, improvised singing and educational practice', *Contemporary Issues in Early Childhood* 7(3): 268–78.

Chapter 7

Playing instruments

Nancy has set up a carpet area with a selection of instruments around her: a xylophone, some individual xylophone bars, some egg shakers, a large rattle and a selection of beaters. She is in a bay area just off a reception classroom. Children join her to play instruments. As they start to play she listens and watches. Sometimes this is enough. Children play a little, they move on to another activity. If it seems welcome and appropriate, Nancy joins in with playing, trying to match her playing as seems best – either imitating by turns, or synchronising her playing. Jasmine plays a group of strikes on the xylophone; it has a clear rhythm and shape to it. Nancy copies it as closely as she can. Jasmine plays again, a phrase of the same length. Nancy imitates her phrase again. This turn-taking continues for a few more turns. Then Jasmine varies it by adding in some drum beats.

This simple two-way game of 'your turn, my turn' and 'do it again exactly or do it again and a little bit different' is a common game format in all kinds of activity and it makes a simple musical structure when played out on instruments. Once playing together with one idea has continued for long enough, it might finish or a contrasting idea is introduced to relaunch it in a new direction. In a study of children's spontaneous play with instruments, I discovered that this kind of children's play is rarely the random, sporadic playing it is often assumed to be, particularly if adults pay it serious attention (Young, 2003a, 2005). The music-making of three- to five-year-olds is full of coherent musical ideas and has components of musical structure. Nancy joined in to help children, when appropriate, to move on from engaging in brief episodes of music play to using musical structure in more sustained and extended periods of music.

She was thus using structured interaction in the medium of music itself as a pedagogical strategy.

Within the kind of activity modelled by Nancy, just as with the playful song activity described in the singing chapter, the children are able to initiate their own play with instruments and the adults judge if and when to join in with playing. All too often, instruments are set out for children's exploratory play, perhaps, if we are honest, with little thought as to which instruments and where and how they might be placed. If the children explore the instruments, they may be left to their own devices with little participation on the part of practitioners to listen, observe and note what the children are doing or to find ways to connect with it and extend it. So we see how Foundation Stage music tends to sit at two ends of a continuum – the adult-initiated, adult-led singing and the child-initiated, child-led free play with instruments. Much of the task of this book is to encourage a wide, varied repertoire of activity, across all the areas of singing, playing and listening, with every shade of shared participation between adult and child.

The expectations of how children will make music with instruments in Foundation Stage curricular documents are, to be frank, very low. Look through the guidance and the emphasis is on children exploring sound rather than discovering how to make music. Young children have the ability, and indeed the imagination and motivation, to shape sounds into musical structures that make musical sense to them and will make sense to us if we listen in the positive expectation that this is music. However, providing good contexts – good 'eliciting and enabling' environments – is the key.

For a start, children quickly pick up which activities in their setting are most valued and which are not. Often the tables neatly arranged with pencil and paper activities are located in the centre of the room and receive high adult attention, and, as the activities move out to the margins, so they receive less attention and are of lower value. One practitioner joked with me that she set the instruments out on shelves down a corridor because 'then the children rarely find them'. Another confessed that she puts out the older, broken instruments for free exploration because, after all, the children just 'biff and bang them'.

Having reflected on these issues, practitioners in one setting laid out instruments in thoughtful selections and arrangements much less frequently than before, but, when they did so, an adult was positioned to listen and be a play partner. The result was that the children played the instruments with more focus – less became more. The attentions of an adult encouraged the children to make music that was shared with the adult listener/player, and the intention to be sociable, to be communicative, generated musical ideas.

THE INSTRUMENTS

So much hinges on the instruments themselves that I discuss these first. It is not only what the children do with the instruments that we need to think about, but also what the instruments *do* for the children? Recent theoretical views on learning place emphasis on the role of 'things' in mediating learning. So, for example, the processes of learning and the potentials for learning are quite different – playing an Orff xylophone with beaters in comparison with, say, a tambourine and triangle.

Instruments need to be the best quality possible. They should sound, look and feel beautiful to handle and play. If handed a wonderful instrument, the first thing we all do is to examine it, try it out and explore its possibilities. Try closing your eyes to listen even more intently.

A long tradition in early years education of providing children with 'one each' for large-group activity has led to the provision of lots of small, low-cost instruments rather than fewer, higher-quality ones. Small instruments are often packed hastily into boxes and trolleys and quickly become tired-looking and tired-sounding. There is still a place for larger-group work requiring a collection of instruments, but in addition there need to be opportunities for children to explore instrumental improvisation and composition in individual and small-group work with instruments that have real musical potential.

There are different groupings of instruments according to the source of vibration:

▶ the whole body of the instrument vibrates – e.g. a woodblock, a cymbal;
▶ the skin vibrates – e.g. a drum;
▶ a string vibrates – e.g. a guitar;
▶ a column of air vibrates – e.g. a whistle;

or the playing actions that produce the sound:

▶ striking the instrument or shaking it;
▶ plucking;

91

▶ scraping or rubbing;

▶ blowing.

Putting economy of production as a priority has resulted in instruments being made of plastics. This may be a hard-wearing, safe material, but if the body of the instrument itself vibrates, the sound may be very poor. Wood, as a general rule, has a better potential for resonance. Economy of production also results in cheap imports and the resultant exploitation of workers. It is now possible to buy 'fair trade' instruments.

Some instruments are tuned – they produce different pitches. Different pitches are produced depending on where you place your fingers on a tin whistle, as with the strings on a guitar, the bars on a xylophone. Other instruments have less of a specific pitch – a maraca or a tambourine, for example, are untuned – although even with untuned instruments it is possible to pick out a sense of the sound being higher pitched or lower pitched. A small drum will probably have a higher-pitched sound than a larger drum. Ensuring that children have access to tuned instruments is important. These tend to be in short supply in early years settings, as do instruments of lower pitch – for the simple reason that they are larger in size and therefore more expensive.

One of the first steps may be to review your instrument selection ensuring range across:

▶ types of instruments and playing actions;

▶ tuned and untuned instruments;

▶ lower as well as higher pitch.

Now add to these hand-played instruments the whole plethora of musical sounds and ways of producing sounds made possible by new technologies, and providing for music-making becomes much more complex – but much more exciting too. New technologies aren't sound-making objects as such; they somehow make invisible the process of producing sound. There are gadgets and gizmos to get excited about, such as leads, microphones, screens, laptops, recording devices, headphones – all manner of paraphernalia. The fact that the production and reproduction of musical sounds is 'magically' hidden inside the equipment means we need to think differently about children's learning when using technology. But this I have already talked about in Chapter 3.

The bonus of technologies is that, freed from needing the playing skills to make the sounds, more – maybe not more, but certainly *different* –

things are possible using technology. For example, there is the way that sound, detached from the actions of making, can become the centre of attention – sound as sound, rather than sound in action. There are pluses and minuses, of course, to using acoustic instruments and using digital equipment – and ways too of combining both. The important thing is to analyse what benefits to children's learning each can bring. The reality is also to emphasise an idea introduced earlier, that digital technologies are a part of contemporary childhoods and we cannot ignore this fact.

'Real' instruments

In accounts of professional musicians recalling significant experiences that started their musical careers, they very often hark back to an occasion when they were able to hear, handle and even have for themselves certain musical instruments (Green, 2002). You may have memories from your own childhood. Opportunities for children to hear and try out instruments, along with hearing the styles of music that are generally played on those instruments, can be profoundly important in starting children on a route into music. Again, this links back with an earlier theme in Chapter 4 on musical neighbourhoods, when we considered the value of visiting musicians in early years settings.

Scrapstore instruments

In early years education, children often make sound-makers and instruments out of scrapstore and recyclable materials. Beyond the value of making, their value for musical learning rests on the same questions as with any acoustic instruments. To what extent are these resources providing potential for imaginative activity with music-learning potential and how pleasing is their sound? One nursery experimented with containers and fillings, listening carefully to find just the right combinations that made pleasing sounds – coarse, dry sand in a metal polish tin; nasturtium seeds in a raffia box. They assembled a whole range of different timbres and pitches in these shakers.

Here are some more illustrative examples. Three-year-olds in Denmark took large plastic drinks bottles 'for a walk' through the woods, dragging them on long ropes like badly behaved dogs. They bounced and bobbed against the trees, making dull bopping noises. This was a sound exploration activity – one that combined outdoor activity with a sense of fun and imagination. Four-year-olds in Italy made a sound cave for the babies in their centre, with suspended teaspoons, tin foil and tissue paper. This required them not only to imagine what was appropriate for the babies, but to select things that sounded well. Five-year-olds on the Isle of Wight investigated the resonance of some metal objects, pieces of piping and cooking utensils, finding ways to suspend them on a clothes frame, deciding what to strike them with. They went on to watch a video of Stomp, a group who make up dance and percussion pieces using everyday and scrapstore items, and created similar dance music themselves.

Sound space for instruments

What kind of sound spaces are available in your setting? Some environments are resonant and seem to amplify the sounds; some have carpets, curtains and furniture that muffle. Bringing music played on instruments into an educational setting can add a new challenge to the sound space. There are a number of practical solutions if noise levels may rise: fewer children at a time, even just one or two, a separate space, out of doors, quieter instruments, special times.

Planning the what, where and when to set out instruments for children to play – the eliciting environments – requires thought. One nursery planned a range of set-ups for single or small collections of instruments and rang the changes weekly. They ensured that their set-ups included a variety of instrumental sounds, ways of playing, opportunities to play alone or with others:

- ▶ two sets of hand-held cymbals in a spacious room with mirrors and some lengths of red and gold fabric for dancing;
- ▶ a basket of Indian bells in different sizes and shapes, so that they made different pitches and slightly different timbres, placed in the entrance way;
- ▶ a selection of differently sized drums and a set of bongos arranged out of doors;
- ▶ an electronic keyboard on a table in a small library room;
- ▶ a guitar or zither (plucked instruments) laid flat on a carpeted area indoors;
- ▶ some blown instruments – saxoflutes, tin whistles, recorders, ocarinas, bamboo pipes – in an interactive activity with an adult;

- a box of shakers and rattles of all kinds, many made of gourds or seed pods; also seed pod and bell anklets, and belts for wearing when dancing in a role-play area;
- a stand with strong clips to hold a range of wood blocks and some wooden and rubber beaters;
- a large resonant drum loaned by a marching band parent and placed outside in the summerhouse for a storytelling activity led by an adult.

The exuberance with which children sometimes play instruments, along with the sheer pleasure in the wash of sound it creates, can be disconcerting, particularly in some settings where there is an unspoken, but nevertheless strictly enforced, restriction on the amount of energy, boisterousness or noise children can display. And loud noises can be very upsetting to some other children. Thoughtfully planned, interesting instrument arrangements, messages of valuing their activity and adult attention can increase the focus. It interests me too that, while many early childhood settings believe in free play, it is often, in reality, freedom within quite narrow boundaries. While the exuberance translated on to paper in painting or thumped out in clay, or even danced, might be welcomed and recognised as children's creative processes, there is often less 'sound room' for children's musical energies. This too might be an issue for reflection and review.

LEARNING TO BE A PLAYER

As with singing, the processes for children learning to be players include being able to listen to good models of playing, being provided with opportunities to play that are appropriate, being encouraged to listen with concentration and to focus on detail and being given encouragement and feedback.

Models of playing

Encouraging children's musical creativity, as with singing, is not only about giving them opportunities to exercise their imaginations, but also about feeding them by providing models. I recently listened to a Brazilian performer – he held what looked like a small, basic, battered tambourine (the pandeiro), but, when he played, it produced the most exciting range of jangles, slaps and trills. He played thumb strokes, and slapped it with

95

the ball of his hand or fingertips to produce interesting variations of timbre and rhythmic patterning. It was captivating. It has completely changed how I look at the humble tambourine now. Lodged in my memory are the sounds and images of him playing.

With many percussion instruments, even the most modest and apparently straightforward to play, attention to how they are handled, held and played can make a huge difference to how well they sound. This is where a moment of focused, direct teaching can be appropriate. A vibrant strike with a hand or beater in just the right part of the instrument can produce a resonant sound instead of a dull thud; plucking in just a certain way, blowing gently, holding the instrument this way or that can all make a difference. This models focused listening and a concern to play with attention to technique so that the sound is the very best we can make it. These listen and play times can be richly descriptive in language to explain playing technique and the sounds that result.

Focusing on the sound itself to encourage perceptive, attentive listening and to feed the aural imagination is a valuable activity and links in closely with Chapter 5 on listening. But it needs to be very challenging. Children are acute and perceptive listeners. As babies they are finely attuned to even the smallest changes in nuance, pitch and inflexion. They have to be, as this is how they connect with the social world around them. So it makes little sense to give children of three years upwards tasks such as differentiating between the sound of a drum and a triangle. This kind of activity may be useful just to teach them the name tags of the instruments but it is not a challenging aural discrimination task:

Cathy takes a pair of Indian bells. Each bell, struck separately, has a slightly different pitch. That is how, when you clash Indian bells together, they make the sound equivalent of biting into a lemon. Holding them apart, she taps one with a small wooden beater and then the other. The children close their eyes and focus on the very slight difference. She plays them again, one after the other, to compare, urging them to hear the tiny difference in pitch.

Niki finds two shaky eggs that have a very slightly different sound – one has slightly more 'filling' than the other. One egg is blue, one is green. She plays them several times over to let the children hear blue and hear green, then hides them behind her back. The children must hear whether the blue one is sounding or the green.

As another example, a similar activity can be developed from a selection of beaters: rubber, felt, wooden. Even rubber beaters are of different densities; some are soft, some are harder. Play the same instrument, perhaps a woodblock, with the different beaters so that the children hear the changing qualities of timbre that the beaters produce.

LIKELY PATTERNS OF INTEREST

When I researched young children's self-initiated play with instruments I discovered different types of playing that might predict likely patterns of interest in the playing of other children (Young, 2003a and b). As with the understandings of children's singing derived from research, I am not suggesting these versions will predict how children play or are set in stone – far from it. But by providing one set of templates they can help with the process of understanding children's music play on instruments, which might otherwise seem random and somewhat disconnected. For another source of information, Jo Glover gives an insightful account of young children's own processes of composing from her own research (Glover, 2000).

Body movements

The music arises from the actions of playing:

> Jason is playing a cymbal on a stand set up in a far corner of the outdoor area. He lifts his arms in a full arc and then brings them down to strike the cymbal. Slowly he repeats this action many times over, swinging his arms in a full circle each time.

The idea of music-making as movement-based or as a series of gestures encourages us to look for these movement ideas and how they are sounded out on the instruments.

Exploring the instrument

The music arises from exploring the different things that the instrument can do:

> Bianca has a guitar, which is laid on the floor. She plucks all the strings one by one, listening acutely to the different pitches. Then she tries

out the fret board, pushing the strings down and sliding her fingers to make quite scratchy sounds with the strings. Then she strums the strings but, finding this a bit painful on some fingers, she tries out different ways of using her fingers to strum. Then she combines plucking the strings with strumming and starts to hum to herself.

Combining instruments

The music arises from different combinations of instruments that are played in sequence:

Lucasz sets out on the floor around him a semicircle of instruments made up of drums and chime-bars. He then plays them one at a time around the semicircle and then back again.

Playing a song

The music arises from a desire to play a song the child already knows or to make up a new song. Playing a tuned, barred instrument is often the stimulus for song and instrument play:

Angel is sitting at a small glockenspiel set up on a table at the side of the classroom. She plays it with small soft rubber beaters, so the sound is quiet and gentle. She plays with a regular beat at a medium tempo, not selecting specific pitches, but as she does so she sings a hello song that the class regularly sing.

Making up a role play

The music arises from a made-up narrative:

Most of the children are outside playing, but Marcus has stayed indoors by the xylophone. He has two large felt-headed beaters and stands these up like puppets. He is making up a story about two people who come home, then go upstairs and do small, everyday things. All the time he is using the beaters to play the xylophone for 'stepping up the stairs' or to 'fall over'.

Playing with someone else

The music arises from collaborating with a friend:

> Bryn is playing a set of bongo drums and some other small percussion
> he has set out around him. Sophie joins him. They don't speak. Bryn
> reaches out a hand to play something on the bongo drums. Then they
> both start to tap the bongo drums, keeping exactly in time with one
> another. Bryn stops. Sophie stops and watches him. He reaches for
> another larger drum. They set it up by the side and then he models
> playing bongos and the larger drum alternately. Sophie copies him.
> They look, they smile. All this time, they have not said a word but
> collaborated through gesture and through sound.

Mixing ideas

As children continue to play they start to mix their ideas, to hybridise
them. Frequently the children's play progresses with a combination of
different ideas. A first playing idea may develop mainly from the action
of playing – body movement ideas. This may then change to a challenge
with playing the instrument itself, tapping the ends of the xylophone or
reaching over to play a nearby drum or adding in a song. Then, as the play
episode continues, they may combine both ideas to make something new.

Chaining and linking

Children also develop their ideas by linking them together in chains. They
will typically repeat something they like, then repeat it with small changes,
and then the changes develop into something further. Perhaps having
played with one idea for a while, they hit on something new. They are
diverted by this new idea. Then, having played with that idea for a while,
they go back to the first, but start to link both ideas up in certain ways.
This is complicated to explain, but once you start to look closely for these
kinds of processes in children's music-making, they become more obvious.

GROUP WORK WITH INSTRUMENTS

There is a long tradition of group work with instruments in early years
practice, whereby each child is handed one instrument each, usually from
a random mix of instruments. They then play along, perhaps to a song or

piece, sometimes to a piece of recorded music. I have memories of a percussion band in 1950s schooling, whereby a large hall of us held a small
instrument each – a triangle, hand drum, tambourine – and played when
directed to recorded music from a gramophone. All I remember was
following a large chart and waiting with anticipation for the moment
when I could 'ting' my triangle.

There are some ways in which larger-group work might be planned
for to avoid the cacophony that can ensue from 'all play at once'. The aim
might be to practise certain playing skills, or how to control the
instruments to play softly, or how to adjust to playing in time at different
speeds. Certain selections of instruments and groupings of children can
improve the resulting sound.

Group instruments to be similar in sound so that they blend:

- all crisp, dry wooden sounds;
- all drums;
- all maracas, dry rattles, shaky eggs;

or have two groups of sound that alternate: wooden sounds, with rattle
sounds. Instruments with resonant metal sounds, such as triangles and
cymbals, often blend less well with other instruments, so they might be
used sparingly.

Restrict the number of instruments and have activities in which
children take turns and pass:

- pass one instrument around (to passing songs and rhymes);
- alternate children have an instrument and pass on;
- one group plays while others sing or move.

Structure the playing:

- Playing the beat might be appropriate, perhaps with two or
  three dry wooden sounds to a lively song, or a deep-sounding
  drum gently played with a soft beater to a slow, quiet song.
- Tapping just a rhythm – pick out the key rhythm from a song
  or piece of music, with children playing only the rhythm when
  it occurs.
- Improvising a pattern to 'fill a gap' in a chant or rhyme, or at
  the end of a song.

▶ Playing instruments to accompany movement. Some children play, some children move: very fast, wild playing for matching movement, then a sudden stop and silence; very slow, ponderous playing on a cymbal for matching movements.

Some approaches to guiding children's play with instruments draw upon visual ideas; typically representations of weather, or a walk. These are often ways to introduce structure – simple structures of rising to a climax and then dying away, or a series of short events linked in some way. The difficulty can be when imagery and narrative ideas take over so that the musical dimension becomes mostly about creating sound effects, sounds that imitate certain things, rather than combine to form music.

There is a subtle but important shift from making sounds to making music.

FURTHER READING

Glover, J. (2000) *Children Composing 4–14*, London: RoutledgeFalmer.

Young, S. (2003) 'Time-space structuring in spontaneous play on educational percussion instruments among three- and four-year-olds', *British Journal of Music Education* 20(1): 45–59.

Chapter 8

Dancing

A class of five-year-olds are working in the classroom. Chairs and tables have been stacked leaving a free, just-big-enough, carpeted space in the middle of the classroom. Annabelle has marked a circle on the floor using insulating tape. She sits on the floor in the circle, watching. The children are dancing freely to some recorded music that has a gentle pace and floating feel to it. When they choose, they can come into the circle and Annabelle will dance with them. Sometimes she echoes and matches the children's movements; sometimes they develop a partner-dance together.

It was a dilemma whether to call this chapter 'Dancing' or 'Moving'. In the end I plumped for 'Dancing', but my concept of dancing includes all kinds of musical movement. Dancing can be thought of as a kind of silent music and music as a kind of noisy dancing. There are musical cultures where there is no separate word in the language for music and dancing – just the one word for both. And in popular culture dance and song are closely integrated. So it is interesting to think why, in our conventional cultural view of music, the body gets separated out into its own art form. Certainly, with young children, the separation seems to make no sense since they make and respond to music in a highly physical way. When they hear music they bounce, they jiggle, they wriggle, sway and swing. They have music in their bones.

Elements of music and dance are closely related. They are two sides of the same coin – speed, rhythm, dynamics and structure can be explored in both media. These ideas of cross-media connection are discussed in the next chapter, where I go on to think about the relationship between music and media such as drawing, using physical objects, words, notation and so on. But music and dance are so closely bound together as to be almost one and the same – a fusion, less a translation, which is why dancing receives more attention in a chapter of its own. Songs and instrumental music that have a strong movement character give inspiration to dance forms and improvised dance. Likewise, movement gives ideas for making music. There are many ways in which activities can flip rapidly between dancing and music.

As with my other 'start of the chapter' examples of practice, this one of Annabelle MacFadyen teaching in a Somerset reception class describes a music-dance environment that has been set up by her to provide a stimulus for children. Annabelle offers to be a dance partner, ready to join in, watching to decide how best to interact with the children, to add to what they are doing.

Physical awareness, or kinaesthetic awareness as it can be termed, is one of our most powerful senses, yet it is often taken for granted. Indeed, interestingly, both the kinaesthetic sense and the sense of balance (for which ears are responsible) are usually not included in the five classic senses. Bodily awareness is in constant use as we move throughout our lives, in and around our environments and with others. To dance music is to gain physical, expressive, emotional experience of it – it's a way of being inside the music, totally immersed – before getting down to the focused skills of performing or analysing or putting it into words and symbols. Thus movement allows for a kind of élan – a holistic involvement in the activity that is learning rich. In earlier chapters I suggested 'movement listening' to recorded music or to live music if other children play or there are performers present. Such activities encourage children to listen actively and represent what they hear in movement. This is a much more accessible way for young children to express and communicate their ideas about music than using words – or indeed, I would suggest, any other media. There can, sometimes, be too much haste to try to get young children to crystallise ideas into words.

Piaget believed that children learn through bodily action – that thought derived from action (see Smidt, 2006: 21–4 for a helpful explanation of Piaget's theories). It is clear then how interest in movement as a medium for learning in music was dominant at around the same time in the 1970s and 1980s as Piaget's theories were having a considerable influence on early childhood education. Movement was seen as the medium through which children could engage in music and experience music, prior to drawing out more formalised understanding from the foundation of their physical experience. There were several research studies that focused on the value of movement-based approaches to music education (e.g. Metz, 1989). However, since then, although music with young children often includes actions or simple movements, the conviction for whole-body movement based on a philosophy and theory of children's learning in music seems to have become less central.

Take a simple concept such as speed – or tempo, to use a musical term. The children run fast. Perhaps as part of a structured activity, perhaps spontaneously out of doors. Now they need to go slowly and cautiously through the mud (as in the *Going on a Bearhunt* story for example) or at a different speed through the long grass. They typically begin their grasp of concepts such as this in relation to their own bodies and senses. Three-year-olds would already have a clear grasp of fast and slow – no need to start with such a simple contrast. So now they are beginning to learn the finer grading of different tempi, but initially in relation to the tempo and movement of their own bodies. One of the theoretical ideas behind moving to music is that, to mobilise the whole body in movement – not just the small extremities of hands or feet tapping, but the body's weight and larger muscle groups – leaves a stronger, more vivid impression on the kinaesthetic memory and thus feeds the rhythmic sense more deeply. At a pop concert, the audience are not neatly tapping their knees, every part of them is on the move.

DANCE SPACE

Just as in talking about instruments, we saw how important it was to think carefully about the selection and provision of good-quality instruments and the sound spaces available, so the same applies to the planning of 'eliciting environments' for dancing. This will include the space, the flooring, any mirrors or props and any recorded music. Spaces in early years settings are often crowded with furniture and things. Even for three-year-olds they start to look like mini-classrooms, with tables and chairs taking out space for moving and playing. What notions of childhood lie behind this kind of environment? Children become very adept at moving with control, poise and expressiveness around the obstacle course that is their indoor environment.

In thinking about music to move to, it is not only what the children do to the music, but what the music can do for them. Here live music can be a bonus because it can be tailored to fit exactly with the children's dancing and a two-way interaction between player and mover can occur. As visiting musicians are increasingly working in early years education and becoming more experienced at how they can integrate their playing into the ongoing activity of the nursery, one strategy is to improvise, responsively, for children's dancing. It is an excellent way, too, in which the children can engage with the musicians' playing.

LEARNING TO BE A DANCER

As children turn three and grow on to five their maturing bodies, increasing in size, strength and motor skills and taking on more 'adult-like' proportions, give them greater scope and possibilities for dancing. They enjoy using their bodies in full motor movement: to run and jump, to gallop, hop if they can, fall down, roll over, slide and squirm. Some children in their lives outside the setting may have ample opportunity and encouragement to move, to dance, to be physically active. Some children, however, are increasingly imprisoned indoors and clamped in car seats and have few opportunities for energetic movement play in outdoor open spaces. So there are additional reasons to provide physical activity. There are some basic skills to introduce:

- ▶ awareness of their own movement in space and the movement of others;
- ▶ stopping and balancing their body weight;
- ▶ body awareness, control, flexibility and coordination;
- ▶ awareness of their movement vocabulary;
- ▶ timing and anticipation.

A repertoire of movement games can introduce these skill-learning aspects in combination with developing awareness of some musical elements.

Movement games

- ▶ *Shake, wriggle and stop!*
  - – Movements on the spot, accompanied by a percussion instrument.
  - – Physical warm up and control.
  - – Sound and silence.

▶ *Move the rhythm pattern.*
  – Make up a simple stamping, stepping or large body-movement pattern.
  – Echo the patterns.
  – Repeat and vary.
  – Perform and recognise rhythm patterns.

▶ *Long movements and long sounds.*
  – Sway gently to long cymbal sounds, feeling their duration.
  – Find a way to measure or count out the long sounds.

▶ *Change for each phrase.*
  – Skip, clap or move on the spot – for one phrase of a song and then change the movement.
  – Recognise phrases.

▶ *Accents.*
  – Feel the stronger beat of the music and then the weaker beat.
  – Find an action to match the strong beat – pull hard, stamp a foot.
  – Sense the pulse and metre of the music.

Dance songs, singing games, action songs

Children's singing and clapping games are typically played in outdoor play spaces. Despite the prevalent idea that children no longer play these kinds of games, researchers interested in children's musical play find that they are alive and well. Kathy Marsh (2008), researching in Keighley and Bedford primary schools, found that playground songs, rhymes, rhythmic movements and chants continue to be played. I mentioned Kathy's research in Chapter 1. What's more, these games are constantly changing, incorporating all kinds of media, popular and multicultural influences from contemporary childhoods. What Kathy has discovered in her careful analysis of these games are two important things for music education. One – that the musical demands are usually much more interesting and challenging than those children were experiencing in their music sessions. (Recall that I found the same thing in relation to children's musical activities in the home.) Two – that they reveal interesting ways in which children learn informally from one another by modelling and by joining in as they can and how more experienced, usually older, children take a lead and help to ease in the novices.

One school pooled its knowledge of children's singing games from all the children and staff, and wrote these on plastic-covered cards to keep in a pocket outdoors. Practitioners could refer to these quickly in initiating singing games. Opening up age-segregated play areas in primary schools can allow the mixing of older children to teach younger children. What Kathy found as well is that individual schools have kinds of 'micro-cultures' and that, where one school had a rich mix of culturally varied singing games, another had very few. She put this down to the school having an explicit multiracial policy, which had soaked deep into school life so that the children felt affirmed in their identity. They felt able to reveal and play with and through their musical identities.

Singing games are rich multimedia forms. They combine melody, dance, drama and rhythmic body percussion in the form of clapping and tapping movements in game formats and mini-narratives. Using singing games in planned, formal class sessions can valuably tap into these characteristics. In my own work I frequently invited five-year-olds to invent their own singing games, either from scratch or from some given starting points.

SPONTANEOUS DANCING

As children move and dance through their lives, there is rhythm and phrasing in their movement. Noticing and thoughtfully observing their spontaneous dance-moving will often reveal these forms of patterning and structure. Like spontaneous singing, children's own dancing often passes unnoticed – or, because children are emulating styles of dancing from popular culture, is dismissed as irrelevant or inappropriate. It may be enough to see and notice, or, as with Annabelle at the start of this chapter, to join in for a moment, to affirm, to draw attention to it by imitating and perhaps commenting. Again, some early childhood professionals will find joining in with dance comes easily to them, while for some it may, literally, be a step they cannot take. The teacher of the reception class in Somerset took inspiration from Annabelle's work and provided for and participated in spontaneous dance and movement activities out of doors using lengths of fabric as a stimulus.

For music learning, the spotlight might focus on cross-over points where the connection between dance and music is closest. Rhythmic patterning, for example, can occur in silent movement as much as in sounded-out versions. Play with materials such as sand, water and clay often stimulates rhythmic movement. Toni Foster, who works across Southampton early years settings, was sitting at a dough table with children coming and going. She made up chants, rhymes and small songs to fit with their dough-play actions. In this way, the children's movement patterns suggested musical patterns – and not the other way around. While there may be a strong tradition of drawing children in, to move in structured ways to songs and games initiated by the adult, the reverse happens much less often. However, starting with movement and adding the music is often a more accessible task for children.

Time, space and energy

Every movement takes place in space. It requires a certain length of time – dependent on the speed and rhythm of the activity – to make the movement in space. And this in turn is dependent on the amount of energy put into the movement. Space, time and the energy, or dynamics, of the movement determine the quality and kind of movement. Take an example. Swing your arm gently to and fro and it draws an arc in space. It swings at a certain pace depending on whether you put only a little energy into it so it lolls to and fro, or whether you put a great deal of energy into it so that it pumps rapidly. There is probably one speed at which it feels most comfortable and natural for you, given your body size, how energetic you feel, your personality.

The important thing here is to recognise that children's bodies are differently proportioned, so the space, time, energy ratios of a child swinging their arm will be different to an adult's. Therefore adults should take care in modelling a movement for children to imitate, particularly in action songs and movement games. It may feel comfortable for 'grown-ups', but may be quite the wrong speed for children's physiques. Observe carefully and, if possible, invite the children to initiate a movement and pick up their timing. Also, a good pace to sing a song does not always coincide with a good pace to act out the actions or movements that go with it. Since much early years song repertoire includes action songs, this is an important consideration. It is probably wise sometimes to sing the song to focus on singing, at a slower pace, and sometimes sing the song to focus on movement, at a faster pace.

Moving in time

When we walk, obviously we walk with a steady regularity. We might slow down or speed up, but we walk steadily. If one leg is hurt, we walk unevenly and it often throws the whole body out of balance. We have a kind of central balancing, an internal sense of pulse, around which we coordinate our bodily movements and actions. A newborn will suck with regularity; a six-month-old will bang its spoon evenly on the high chair.

Children (unless they have a disability) have no difficulty performing actions with a steady beat. So the skill and drill steady-beat activities that are often recommended for early years practice are merely consolidating a skill children already possess and are serving no learning purpose. The skill some children may need help with learning is to be able to adjust their speed – their tempo – to keep in time with others. This involves relating their internal sense of pulse to, and adjusting it to match, what we see or hear outside ourselves.

To make these adjustments may be particularly challenging at the extremes of tempo – slower and faster than children normally perform movements. Ask a group of young children to perform a movement quickly, and the excitement levels rise and the lack of control can tip into wildness. Ask them to do it very slowly, and they find the balance and coordination difficult. No reason to avoid these two extremes – in fact, this is where children need the practice. If anything, musical activities in early years settings tend to gravitate to a speed zone of not-too-fast and not-too-slow – and not-very-interesting musically therefore.

One of the principles of music and movement work is for the children to initiate a movement and then to fit the music, the song or an instrument you are playing to the tempo of their movement. Thus the children are setting their own movement tempo and the music adjusts to them, rather than vice versa. Margareta Burrell works at the Thomas Coram Children's Centre, London. She invited a class of three- and four-year-olds to 'go for a walk' with her, in silence, except for the patter of bare feet on smooth wooden floor. Closely watching the speed at which they started to walk, she picked up their average tempo, drumming lightly on a small hand drum. She observed them all intently, telling some if they need to go a little faster or slower to 'fit with my drum'. 'Stop!' she called. 'Now can someone show me much slower walking?' The tempo changed and, again, Margareta's playing picked up this new tempo. In this activity the children heard the sound adjusting to their movement and thus could experience the synchrony between tempo sensed kinaesthetically and tempo sensed aurally.

Body percussion

Body percussion activities, from the simplest clapping to quite complex patterns of stamping and tapping different parts of the body, are a valuable way to encourage musical engagement. Traditional folk styles or contemporary styles of dancing quite often include percussive movements – even tap dancing could be thought of as a kind of body percussion. Children's clapping games frequently include quite challenging patterns – the physical equivalent of tongue-twisters.

The only caution with body percussion is that overuse of clapping and tapping patterns in work with children can become tiring on the ear and body. Rhythmic movement does not need to make a sound – to 'percuss' – in order to enact the rhythm. Indeed, movements to enact rhythm patterns may represent them more accurately as they actually occur in sound if they show the duration of sounds rather than the moment of impact. A long sound, for example – if clapped – could be mistaken for just a short sound with a long silence. Better, often, to act out rhythms with continuous, sliding or stroking hand movements, or arm movements that emphasise the duration.

TO SUM UP

In this chapter I have covered several different aspects of moving and dancing as they relate to music and to music learning among young children. The chapter focused on children's spontaneous dancing, on dancing to music and on some specific detail of learning to match movement to music.

FURTHER READING

Marsh, K. (2008) *The Musical Playground: global tradition and change in children's songs and games*, Oxford: Oxford University Press.

Chapter 9

Into other modes

Music is invisible and it doesn't stay still. Difficult stuff, then, to pin down and learn about. Looking across the whole of early years education, much of what children do and learn focuses on visible and solid things that do obligingly stay still. When they paint, or make something, the results of their activity are fixed, on paper, in clay or in other materials.

Early years settings in the UK are full of things. Objects are set out, played with, looked at, explored, talked about, drawn on paper. Ideas are strongly rooted in the concrete or in their visual images. Even when ideas are more abstract, they are often pulled back into visual representation. Children might be invited to create music but more often than not they are given a visual image as stimulus. Perhaps the stimulus is to make music about the weather, the rainforest, animals or the sea. They are rarely invited to make up music around aural ideas, such as contrasts of metal and wood sounds, or to experiment with quiet long sounds, or with time-based, structural ideas, such as making shared music with a partner, or music for two dancing children.

Music is a particular challenge then – in comparison with other areas of the early years curriculum – because it is primarily an aural medium. There are two approaches for working in music to develop children's understanding. One is to find ways of working with music that recognise that it is aural, abstract and time-based, and emphasise the listening, the musical thinking and understanding of time-based processes that this will involve. This I have tried to do at various points throughout this book. Music happens in time, events unfold, in sequence. What comes first affects what will come next, which then suggests what might come after that. It is holding on to sequential ideas in our minds, intangible strings of ideas,

111

narratives that follow one thing on to another, that underpins much learning and much creativity. Being able to hold in mind how things have unfolded and imagine how they might unfold next – to think ahead – is a fundamental ability.

The second approach is to find ways of working with music that convert it into other media, transforming aural ideas into visual representations, into gestures, movements and sometimes, too, words. Converting music into other media will pick out certain features of the music and make them easier to share and understand. For example, a rhythm pattern mapped out in small bricks on the floor will pick out the number of beats exactly and could show how long they last for. The conversion will also leave out some features of the music. The bricks cannot show how fast the rhythm pattern goes, or what instrument plays it, or how loud it might be. But the brick-rhythms do allow certain focused discussions to develop more easily than might be the case with rhythms that exist only in sound. So it is a process of transforming that highlights some features at the expense of others, not of translating exactly. This slipping from mode to mode is something that children do intuitively in their own self-generated playful activity and it has been of interest to many researchers looking closely at children's activity in other areas (e.g. Kress, 1997). So children are strongly inclined to transform and see connections between different modes and we can take full advantage of this.

Tapping into children's abilities for cross-modal – or analogical – thinking is not only a means to extend children's musical understanding, it is also a powerful means to develop imagination. Kress refers to the 'dynamic interaction between modes' (Kress, 1997: 154), whereby the process of changing musical ideas from one form to another generates ideas and makes possible new connections and relationships. So, once the bricks represent the rhythm pattern, they can start to be moved around and the patterns developed. These are processes that are identified as broad behaviours that children demonstrate when they are being creative. They can happen in the smallest moments as this next example shows:

Three-year-old Amalie is settling into the nursery. She is holding a brown, felt-tip pen. She makes a small dot on Madeline's arm. 'Bop!' says Madeline, quickly and quietly, in such a way that exactly mirrors the little action of making the dot. Amalie dots about six dots on Madeline's arm in a little group. Madeline vocalises 'bop, bop' with each dot. There is a long pause. Amalie draws a circle and looks up, waiting. 'Whoop!' vocalises Madeline. So does Amalie. Madeline draws circles and dots; Amalie voices the whoops and bops.

Such a simple, small activity with a cautious three-year-old (who rarely speaks in nursery because English is not her first language) may be over very quickly. But for Amalie these small groupings of dots are acted out, seen and heard. Intuitively she will have recognised the relationship between the visual and aural modes, heard and seen simultaneously in a tiny activity, over in a moment. There were no words spoken here – communication was by gesture, by eye contact, by implicit understanding. Throughout this book I am emphasising that interaction in music learning, dialogue and communication with young children may well not involve talking about it – but clearly using words is a very important pedagogical strategy and deserves thoughtful attention.

TALKING ABOUT MUSIC

Vygotsky (1962) proposed that language is central to learning and that the interrelationship between thinking, talking and learning is essential. The process of talking gives substance to thinking. In a reflective seminar, which was part of a recent music project in Birmingham, we analysed the way a group of three music practitioners working in early years settings had used talk in their work with young children. We took short video clips selected from their recent working in children's centres. We reviewed them several times, listening, thinking and analysing. Each practitioner had a different style. One hardly spoke at all, but worked almost entirely through music, through facial expression and gesture – 'unspoken words'. On this occasion she was working with three-year-olds, many of whom did not have English as their first language, so her style was entirely appropriate. Another, with older children, kept up an almost constant dialogue, naming, suggesting, instructing. It was an activity of exploring instrumental sounds that needed a lot of interactive structuring, prompting and assistance on her part. A third was working in creative improvisation with two children and instruments. During the course of this activity the children commented, spontaneously at certain points, and she responded by echoing their words but did not attempt to develop any kind of verbal dialogue, preferring to focus on the musical dialogue. Children becoming aware, thinking, developing understanding – all components of learning – are dependent on the quality of dialogue with adults and the subtlety of the adult participation. Important then that we give it due attention and don't leave it to routine or chance.

We went on to discuss questioning – analysing how they had used questions and going on to consider how they might use questions productively in their future work. Across education as a whole, not just in music, there is a tendency to ask questions of children as a means of focusing their attention, or for simple recall of factual information. These 'educational' questions can be somewhat artificial and not like the kinds of conversations parents or family members might have with children. Because so much questioning is of this closed and non-productive type, it has been criticised. Open-ended questions can be a useful way to check children's understanding – a means to access what they already know and to clarify ideas. Questions can also be asked to prompt children to think and to offer their ideas – 'What might happen?', 'What do you think?', 'What if?' These kinds of open-ended, genuinely enquiring questions foster creative thinking. Equally, sometimes, rather than ask questions, it can be valuable simply to tell the children something new or to describe the activity, and in these ways to model and provide a vocabulary for talking about music. The aim is to stimulate the children's active language through which to develop their musical thinking, understanding and imagination.

In a nutshell talk can be used to:

- ▶ focus attention and excite interest;
- ▶ give vocabulary – name, label and describe;
- ▶ give information and instructions;
- ▶ model ways of talking about music;
- ▶ suggest and prompt;
- ▶ help children to reflect;
- ▶ involve children in discussion so that they learn;
- ▶ encourage curiosity and motivation to investigate;
- ▶ help children to organise their ideas and to have new ideas;
- ▶ ask to check understanding.

When children offer ideas, opinions or suggestions, 'revoicing' – a technique of repeating what a child has said – can be valuable. In this way, the adult clarifies, confirms the importance of what the child has said and can go on to make connections with something else the child might have encountered or something new. This way of using language is very similar to the process of playing with children on instruments and 'revoicing' what the child has just played by imitating it. It links too with the EPPE Project's finding that 'thematic conversations' were an effective pedagogical strategy.

Giving feedback to children, to evaluate their contributions, is also a very well-established part of early years practice. We do children a disservice, it seems to me, if we offer enthusiastic praise routinely so that it becomes shallow. To be genuinely part of holding high expectations of children, feedback should be tailored to task and achievement. 'I could see you were all listening carefully that time. Let's do it one more time and tell me if you can hear the difference between these two sounds.' 'I listened to you all singing and almost everyone is singing the last part of the tune with the right melody, but are some of you still finding the end bit hard?' Far from destroying children's musical self-esteem, such feedback conveys a strong sense of being concerned that children do things well, that they will work at things, learn and progress. Also, it invites children to think how they are doing themselves – a process of learning to evaluate their own learning. Margaret Carr (2001) has given thought to children's learning dispositions and how adults can encourage children to become resilient as learners – to persist in the face of setbacks. Thoughtful and well-tailored feedback is part of that process. It contributes, too, to the 'cognitive challenge' that the EPPE Project suggests is often lacking in early years education.

Words

There are many different relationships of words to musical activity: words to give names to different things happening in the music – loud and soft, fast and slow, ending, beginning, rhythm pattern and so on; or descriptive words and onomatopoeic word sounds that evoke certain qualities and characteristics of the music and start to have a music all of their own. Word play blends with voice play and blends with song. When Jack and Joel acted out their *Thunderbirds* play, the words became a kind of music drama in which words, voice-use and song merged.

Words, particularly in poetry, have a natural rhythm to them. Spoken, then chanted, they can then be played to sound out as music. Taking rhythm patterns from songs and chanting the words to reinforce them can work well, however. Word chanting and rapping are popular activities for which there are some excellent published examples available.

Numbers

Much music in the world is organised around beats that are then counted out into larger groups or units. This might be regular groups of 2, 3 or 4 as in much Western music. Or it might be combinations of different groupings to arrive at interesting irregular rhythms. Jane invited the children to sit cross-legged and then tap the floor on 1 and tap their knees on 2. Next they tapped the floor on 1 and their knees on 2–3, and so on with 4 counts or more. With the reception class she went on to invite them to make up patterns of groups, 2 followed by 3 for example.

The regularity with which we are so familiar in Western music is only one way of organising rhythm and frankly is not the most exciting! There are styles of music where the beats are accented in off-beat ways or grouped irregularly, musics where beats are not all the same length, but some longer than others. Some musics have long cyclical groupings of beats that come around after 16 beats or more. Older children can be challenged to strike a gong or resonant cymbal and then count cycles of 4, 8 or 16 beats before striking again.

Letters

Letters are used in the European system for identifying fixed pitches. Most people know about finding 'middle C' on the piano, and the seven-note scale runs from A to G. Most tuned educational percussion instruments have the letters on the keys for each pitch. Children are usually interested in these letterings and some older children, when making up music on tuned percussion, will write out their melodies using these letters. They also like to 'decode' secret musical messages given to them as a series of letters.

Rhythm syllables

The use of nonsense syllables to match rhythmic and melodic patterning is almost an automatic way of conveying 'how the music goes' to someone else – dum, dum-di, du – um. And syllables might pick up something of the sound quality of the instrument – its timbre – 'ting, ting, ting – scrrritch'. When working with children, nonsense syllables can be a direct way of communicating musical ideas, with added sense of fun. Rhythmic patterning converts very easily into syllable sounds and helps to etch out and clarify the rhythm for the children to grasp. In some musical systems and in some approaches to teaching music these have been formalised.

Southern Indian musicians use rhythmic syllables: Ta, Taka, Takita, Takadimi. Try them. These syllables feel good in the mouth. They are a kind of mouth percussion. Some music education methods use what are known as French time names: Ta, Ta Te, Tafatefi.

The value of such systems of rhythm syllables lies in the fact that, if they are applied consistently, regularly and progressively, then the children become familiar with them and can use them independently. A little and often, as a quick warm-up or to get everyone back into focus and concentrate, can be valuable. The downside is that they can quickly become routine and wooden, perhaps losing touch with a genuine, music-learning purpose.

Pitch syllables

Syllables for pitch names have been around for a long time, the common doh, re, mi, fah, soh, la, ti, doh having been used in European music since about 1600. In India syllables are attached to seven pitches in ascending order – sa, re, ga, ma, pa, dha, ni, sa.

Some approaches to early years music education, particularly approaches derived from the methods known as Kodàly and Kindermusik, recommend introducing the solfa syllables, usually starting with two syllables such as soh and mi and gradually introducing more. It is valuable to know that these approaches have as a principle the introduction of children to formal Western notation. If that is an aim, perhaps as part of a structured programme that will lead to instrumental tuition, then such structured sequential learning can be valuable.

THINGS

Using objects or material that can be moulded, such as dough or clay, to represent aspects of the music – to do with time, to do with pitch or to do with structure – has a particular advantage. The objects or stuff can be laid out, moved around and changed as the thinking takes place. Trial and error and exploring ideas become possible. Making marks, once pencil has touched paper, are fixed.

Small construction equipment or natural objects, such as pebbles, twigs, seed pods or dried beans, are particularly useful for mapping out patterns of beats or units of rhythm. Try threading beads into rhythm patterns. Strings and ropes can map out melodic shapes, or longer sequences such as phrasing. Sandpits or outdoor muddy areas can be moulded and scratched to form shapes. In one school, I used to work in a hall and found the gym equipment, hoops, beanbags, bats and mats all useful objects for making architectures of how the music sounds. Another advantage of large-scale equipment is that pathways and islands can be made, and these can then be 'travelled'; stepped, danced, crawled or slithered along as the music is played or sung.

DRAWING

Drawing to music is frequently suggested as a valuable activity to focus children's attention when listening to recorded music. In my experience I find that, almost invariably, the activity of drawing takes over from the listening so that what is represented on paper does not match what is happening in the music. The confluence between the two media of drawing and listening to music seems, to me, the least successful out of all the possible media 'overlaps'. Certainly with the youngest children, it is a difficult concept to grasp that they are representing something about the music in their drawing.

With the oldest children in this age phase – those nearing five, it is possible to suggest mark-making on paper as a way of focusing attention on musical detail. In a previous book, Jo Glover and I listed different kinds of notation that children might begin to use in order to record or represent the music (Young and Glover, 1998: 99). We took examples from our own teaching and, in addition, examples from research studies. At first, children usually draw the instrument itself or perhaps their hands. This reflects their initial focus on the activity of making the sound – rather than being able to detach the sound from the act of making. With older children this might progress to making a series of marks or tallies to denote a number of strikes or beats, or different playing actions.

Grids and charts

Many forms of conventional notation are written in grids or on systems of lines. Particularly with reception-age children, such notations can be approached as interesting puzzles, both to decode and make up. The key things to learn at this stage are that there is a relationship between certain aspects of the music – the pitch relationships, the duration relationships – that can be converted into little blobs and dots in interesting, logical arrangements on the grids, lines, boxes and so on. Whether the children decide upon the relationships between sound and symbol for themselves, or learn conventional relationships, will depend on the directions their learning is taking and what their current needs are.

Giving children examples of notations to look at – songbooks with the notation written in them, guitar tablature, drum notation, for example – arouses their interest and curiosity. I recently noticed three children standing at a piano with a songbook on the stand. They were turning the pages to find assembly songs they knew, and 'playing' them on the piano, singing along.

GESTURES

Thinking about the way that sound and gesture blend connects with the last chapter on dancing. Here we can pause to think about the way that gesture can specifically represent certain musical elements. Gestures or small movements can convey all kinds of rhythmic and expressive detail. You only have to watch a conductor to understand this well. Timbre, dynamics and the expressive qualities of music can be conveyed through bodily movement.

Gestures can be used to help to reinforce aspects of pitch learning. The relationships between higher-pitched sounds and lower-pitched sounds always take children quite a lot of experience to grasp. This is because the labelling of pitches as 'high' and 'low' are arbitrary. The pitch sounds are often described by children as loud (low) and soft (high). Therefore, to act out the movement of melodies with movements that are spatially higher and lower helps children to learn this connection. In teaching songs to four- and five-year-olds, it can be helpful to map out with simple gestures how the melody moves (and also describe in words), particularly if the learning purpose is to focus on helping the children to match the pitch of a given song. The solfa system has a series of hand signs associated with it that are sometimes used to help develop children's understanding of pitch.

TO SUM UP

This chapter has looked at the many different ways in which music can blend, fuse and morph into other media in order to extend, enhance and enrich children's musical experience and learning.

FURTHER READING

Kress, G. (1997) *Before Writing: rethinking the paths to literacy*, London: Routledge.

To end

What is it that distinguishes the superficial exploration of instruments from something that holds our attention? What is it that captures our imagination when a child sings a made-up song of her own? What is it that feels so right, so pleasing and uplifting when we dance with children to a lively piece of folk music?

There is an impossible-to-define quality about working with young children musically in child-centred, creative ways – a tentativeness that allows the imagination of childhood, the thrill of exploration and vitality, their humour and their spontaneity to become centre stage. Important work.

References

Abbott, L. and Nutbrown, C. (eds) (2001) *Experiencing Reggio Emilia: implications for pre-school provision*, Buckingham: Open University Press.

Addessi, A.R. and Pachet, F. (2005) 'Experiment with a musical machine: style replication in 3/5 year old children', *British Journal of Music Education* 22(1): 21–46.

Campbell, P. Shehan (1998) *Songs in their Heads: music and its meaning in children's lives*, Oxford: Oxford University Press.

Campbell, P. Shehan (2004) *Teaching Music Globally: experiencing music, expressing culture*, Oxford: Oxford University Press.

Carr, M. (2001) *Assessment in Early Childhood Settings: learning stories*, London: Paul Chapman Publishing.

Clark, A. and Moss, P. (2001) *Listening to Young Children: the mosaic approach*, London: National Children's Bureau.

Craft, A., Jeffrey, B. and Leibling, M. (eds) (2001) *Creativity in Education*, London: Continuum.

Davies, C. (1992) '"Listen to my song": a study of songs invented by children aged from 5 to 7 years', *British Journal of Music Education* 9(1): 19–48.

Dweck, C. (2000) *Self Theories: their role in motivation, personality and development*, Philadelphia, PA: Taylor and Francis.

Glover, J. (2000) *Children Composing 4–14*, London: RoutledgeFalmer.

Green, L. (2002) *How Popular Musicians Learn: a way ahead for music education*, Aldershot: Ashgate.

Hsee, Y. and Rutkowski, J. (2006) 'Early musical experience in touch with general human development: an investigation of Vygotsky's scaffolding in music lessons for preschoolers', in L. Suthers (ed.) *Touched by Musical Discovery, Disciplinary and Cultural Perspectives: proceedings of the ISME Early Childhood Music Education Commission Seminar, July 9–14,* Taiwan: Chinese Cultural University Taipei, pp. 112–20.

Kress, G. (1997) *Before Writing: rethinking the paths to literacy,* London: Routledge.

McPherson, G.E. and Davidson, J.W. (2006) 'Playing an instrument', in G.E. McPherson (ed.) *The Child as Musician: a handbook of musical development,* Oxford: Oxford University Press.

Marsh, J. (2005) 'Media, popular culture and young children', in J. Weinberger, C. Pickstone and P. Hannon (eds) *Learning from Sure Start: working with young children and their families,* Maidenhead: Open University Press.

Marsh, K. (2008) *The Musical Playground: global tradition and change in children's songs and games,* Oxford: Oxford University Press.

Marsh, K. and Young, S. (2006) 'Musical play', in G.E. McPherson (ed.) *The Child as Musician: a handbook of musical development,* Oxford: Oxford University Press, pp. 289–310.

Metz, E. (1989) 'Movement as a musical response among preschool children', *Journal of Research in Music Education* 37(1): 48–60.

Nyrop, D. (2006) 'Micro-pedagogy: inside a teacher's head', workshop presented at the ISME Early Childhood Music Education Commission Seminar, Chinese Cultural University Taipei, Taiwan, July 9–14.

Pond, D. (1981) 'A composer's study of young children's innate musicality', *Bulletin of the Council for Research in Music Education* 68: 1–12.

Rutkowski, J. and Runfola, M. (eds) (2007) *Tips: the child voice,* 2nd edn, Lanham, MA: Rowman and Littlefield.

Rutkowski, J. and Trollinger, V. (2005) 'Experiences: singing', in J.W. Flohr (ed.) *The Musical Lives of Young Children,* Upper Saddle River, NJ: Pearson, Prentice Hall, pp. 78–97.

Schön, D. (1987) *Educating the Reflective Practitioner,* San Francisco, CA: Jossey-Bass.

Sims, W. (1986) 'The effect of high versus low teacher affect and active versus low student activity during music listening on preschool children's attention, piece preference, time spent listening, and piece recognition', *Journal of Research in Music Education* 34(2): 173–91.

Siraj-Blatchford, I., Sylva, K., Muttock, S., Gilden, R. and Bell, D. (2002) *Researching Effective Pedagogy in the Early Years* (REPEY), DfES Research Report 356, London: DfES/HMSO.

Smidt, S. (2006) *The Developing Child in the 21st Century: a global perspective on child development*, Oxon: Routledge.

Sundin, B. (1998) 'Musical creativity in the first six years', in B. Sundin, G.E. McPherson and G. Folkestad (eds) *Children Composing: research in music education 1998: 1*, Lund, Sweden: Malmö Academy of Music, Lund University, pp. 35–56.

Sylva, K., Melhiush, E.C., Sammons, P., Siraj-Blatchford, I. and Taggart, B. (2004) *EPPE, Technical Paper 12 – The Final Report, Effective Pre-school Education*, London: DfES/ Institute of Education, University of London.

Vygotsky, L.S. (1962) *Thought and Language*, Cambridge, MA: MIT Press.

Vygotsky, L.S. (1987) *The Collected Works of L.S.Vygotsky*, New York: Plenum Press.

Welch, G. (2006) 'Singing and vocal development', in G.E. McPherson (ed.) *The Child as Musician: a handbook of musical development*, Oxford: Oxford University Press, pp. 311–29.

Young, S. (1995) 'Listening to the music of early childhood', *British Journal of Music Education* 12(1): 51–8.

Young, S. (2002) 'Young children's spontaneous vocalisations in free play: observations of two- to three-year-olds in a day-care setting', *Bulletin of the Council for Research in Music Education* 152: 43–53.

Young, S. (2003a) *Music with the Under Fours*, London: RoutledgeFalmer.

Young, S. (2003b) 'Time-space structuring in spontaneous play on educational percussion instruments among three- and four-year-olds', *British Journal of Music Education* 20(1): 45–59.

Young, S. (2005) 'Musical communication between adults and young children', in D. Miell, R. McDonald and D.J. Hargreaves (eds) *Musical Communication*, Oxford: Oxford University Press.

Young, S. (2006) 'Seen but not heard: young children, improvised singing and educational practice', *Contemporary Issues in Early Childhood* 7(3): 268–78.

Young, S. (2007) 'Digital technologies, young children, and music education practice', in K. Smithrim and R. Upitis (eds) *Listen to their Voices: research and practice in early childhood music*, Toronto: Canadian Music Educators Association.

Young, S. and Glover, J. (1998) *Music in the Early Years*, London: The Falmer Press.

Index

eBooks – at www.eBookstore.tandf.co.uk

A library at your fingertips!

eBooks are electronic versions of printed books. You can store them on your PC/laptop or browse them online.

They have advantages for anyone needing rapid access to a wide variety of published, copyright information.

eBooks can help your research by enabling you to bookmark chapters, annotate text and use instant searches to find specific words or phrases. Several eBook files would fit on even a small laptop or PDA.

NEW: Save money by eSubscribing: cheap, online access to any eBook for as long as you need it.

Annual subscription packages

We now offer special low-cost bulk subscriptions to packages of eBooks in certain subject areas. These are available to libraries or to individuals.

For more information please contact webmaster.ebooks@tandf.co.uk

We're continually developing the eBook concept, so keep up to date by visiting the website.

www.eBookstore.tandf.co.uk